10
Pocket
Positives

1000
Pocket
Positives

Inspiring quotations to
enlighten, refresh and uplift

COMPILED BY
JAN SUTTON

howtobooks

Published by How To Books Ltd,
3 Newtec Place, Magdalen Road,
Oxford OX4 1RE. United Kingdom.
Tel: (01865) 793806. Fax: (01865) 248780.
email: info@howtobooks.co.uk
http://www.howtobooks.co.uk

First edition 2003

British Library Cataloguing in Publication Data.
A catalogue record for this book is available from
the British Library.

Cover design by Baseline Arts Ltd, Oxford
Produced for How To Books by Deer Park Productions
Typeset by Pantek Arts Ltd, Maidstone, Kent
Printed and bound by Bell & Bain Ltd, Glasgow

Contents

Dedicated to Daniel, Rosie and Mia
my cherished grandchildren

Nobody can do for little children what grandparents do.
Grandparents sort of sprinkle stardust over the lives of little children.
Alex Haley (1921–1992) US writer

*A special word of gratitude to my dear friends Claire from the
UK, and Shel from the USA, for their valued support,
feedback, and assistance with research. Also, my thanks to
Giles and Nikki at How To Books, for giving me the
opportunity to compile the book, and to Penny, my friend, for
her help with proofreading. Finally, my heartfelt appreciation
to my husband, Gordon, for his assistance with proofreading,
his patience, and, most importantly, for being there.*

Can miles truly separate us from friends?
If we want to be with someone we love, aren't we already there?
Richard Bach (1936–) US writer

Husbands are like fires. They go out if unattended.
Zsa Zsa Gabor (1917–) Hungarian-born US actress

Introduction

Collecting wise and witty quotes has been an absorbing passion of mine
for several years. Hence I was over the moon when *How to Books*
invited me to compile a book of 1000 inspiring quotes. Bringing this
book together has been a rewarding experience, and throughout the
project, my focus has remained firmly fixed on quality rather than
quantity. The captivating nuggets of wisdom and wit brought together
here come from ancient and modern authors, as well as the famous,
infamous, and not so famous. Some amusing quotes designed to raise a
hearty chuckle have been included. Conversely, there are also quotes
covering a range of issues of a more serious nature such as suicide,
death and dying, and divorce. Men and women with psychological
problems, who often demonstrate a remarkable capacity to laugh at
themselves and their difficulties, drew some of the quotes listed under
'mental health' to my attention. A few anonymous quotes, deemed too
good to omit, have also been incorporated.

Many of the quotes included in the book are personal favourites that
have etched their way into my memory and have played a key role in
my self-development. Similarly, some have provided inspiration in my
work as a counsellor, author and trainer. My hope is that the book will
enlighten, educate, entertain, and encourage personal growth.
Moreover, may it act as a guiding light when you require an insightful
or humourous quotation to add sparkle to your articles, essays,
speeches, presentations, handouts, or websites, or when your own
spirits need uplifting.

During the compilation stage, careful attention was given to accurately
presenting the quotations, proper sources, and author details. In a
venture such as this, however, the odd mistake is not unheard of.
Should you discover any errors or are able to provide information on
anonymous quotes that remain without acknowledgement, please
contact the publishers at info@howtobooks.co.uk. Constructive
feedback is always welcome too.

How to use this book

User friendliness was also given precedence when deciding how best to arrange the book. You will find quotes containing similar words, or themes, grouped together – for example: *Attitude, beliefs, thinking and thought; books and diaries,* and *compliments, encouragement and praise.* Quotes within each section are arranged alphabetically. The sequence of entries within each section is by alphabetical order of quotations. The author index provides brief individual biographical information as well as the author's quotation number(s). Finally, the subject index directs you to specific topics and important keywords.

Jan Sutton, 2003

Maxims and aphorisms,
let us remember that wisdom is the true salt of literature,
and the books that are most nourishing are richly stored with it,
and that is the main object to seek in reading books.

John Morley (1838–1923) English journalist, politician, historian

Abilities, intelligence, genius and talent

Abilities

1. Ability may get you to the top, but it takes character to keep you there.
   John Wooden

2. Great ability develops and reveals itself increasingly with every new assignment.
   Baltasar Gracian

3. It is a fine thing to have ability, but the ability to discover ability in others is the true test.
   Elbert Hubbard

4. Natural abilities are like natural plants; they need pruning by study.
   Francis Bacon

5. The difference between what we do and what we are capable of doing would suffice to solve most of the world's problems.
   Mahatma Gandhi

6. To know how to hide one's ability is great skill.
   François La Rochefoucauld

7. When love and skill work together, expect a masterpiece.
   John Ruskin

Intelligence

8. Intelligence is quickness to apprehend as distinct from ability, which is capacity to act wisely on the thing apprehended.
   Alfred North Whitehead

Genius

9. Genius is merely a greater aptitude for patience.
    Georges-Louis Leclerc Buffon

10. Genius is one percent inspiration and ninety-nine percent perspiration.
    Thomas Edison

11. If there be anything that can be called genius, it consists chiefly in ability to give that attention to a subject which keeps it steadily in the mind, till we have surveyed it accurately on all sides.
    Theodor Reik

12. The secret of genius is to carry the spirit of the child into old age, which means never losing your enthusiasm.
    Aldous Huxley

Talent

13. Everyone has talent. What is rare is the courage to follow the talent to the dark place where it leads.
    Erica Jong

14. Hide not your talents. They for use were made. What's a sundial in the shade?
    Benjamin Franklin

15. Those who are blessed with the most talent don't necessarily outperform everyone else. It's the people with follow-through who excel.
    Mary Kay Ash

16. Use what talents you possess: the woods would be very silent if no birds sang there except those that sang best.
    Henry van Dyke

Absence

17   Never part without loving words to think of during your absence.
It may be that you will not meet again in this life.
Jean Paul Richter

18.   The joy of life is variety; the tenderest love requires to be
renewed by intervals of absence.
Samuel Johnson

19.   The longest absence is less perilous to love than the terrible
trials of incessant proximity.
Ouida

Abstinence and excess

Abstinence

20.   I feel sorry for people who don't drink. When they wake up in
the morning, that's as good as they're going to feel all day.
Frank Sinatra

21.   If you resolve to give up smoking, drinking and loving, you
don't actually live longer; it just seems longer.
Clement Freud

Excess

22.   The road of excess leads to the palace of wisdom.
William Blake

Acceptance

23.   Acceptance of one's life has nothing to do with resignation; it
does not mean running away from the struggle. On the contrary,
it means accepting it as it comes, with all the handicaps of
heredity, of suffering, of psychological complexes and injustices.
Paul Tournier

24. Acceptance of what has happened is the first step to overcoming the consequences of any misfortune.
William James

25. At the heart of personality is the need to feel a sense of being lovable without having to qualify for that acceptance.
Paul Tournier

26. God grant me the serenity
To accept the things I cannot change,
Courage to change the things I can,
And wisdom to know the difference.
Serenity Prayer used by Alcoholics Anonymous
Reinhold Niebuhr

27. It is no good casting out devils. They belong to us, we must accept them and be at peace with them.
D. H. Lawrence

28. The greatest gift that you can give to others is the gift of unconditional love and acceptance.
Brian Tracy

29. We cannot change anything until we accept it. Condemnation does not liberate, it oppresses.
Carl Gustav Jung

Accomplishments, achievements and satisfaction

Accomplishments

30. I long to accomplish a great and noble task, but it is my chief duty to accomplish small tasks as if they were great and noble.
Helen Keller

31. It is amazing what you can accomplish if you do not care who gets the credit.
Harry S. Truman

32. To accomplish great things, we must not only act, but also dream: not only plan, but also believe.
    Anatole France

Achievements

33. Achievement brings its own anticlimax.
    Maya Angelou

34. Four steps to achievement: plan purposefully, prepare prayerfully, proceed positively, pursue persistently.
    William Arthur Ward

35. If I have seen further than others, it is because I have stood on the shoulders of giants.
    Isaac Newton

36. There isn't a person anywhere that isn't capable of doing more than he thinks he can.
    Henry Ford

37. Those who dare to fail miserably can achieve greatly.
    Robert F. Kennedy

Satisfaction

38. Look at a day when you are supremely satisfied at the end. It's not a day when you lounge around doing nothing. It's when you've had everything to do, and you've done it.
    Margaret Thatcher

39. To be able to look back upon one's past life with satisfaction is to live twice.
    Lord Acton

Action, deeds and doubts

Action

40. Always behave like a duck – keep calm and unruffled on the surface but paddle like the devil underneath.
    Jacob M. Braude

41. Do what you can with what you have where you are.
Theodore Roosevelt

42. I am always doing things I can't do, that's how I get to do them.
Pablo Picasso

43. I hear and I forget, I see and I remember, I do and I understand.
Chinese proverb

44. Take time to deliberate; but when the time for action arrives, stop thinking and go in.
Andrew Jackson

45. The "as if" principle works. Act "as if" you were not afraid and you will become courageous, "as if" you could and you'll find you can. Act "as if" you like a person and you'll find a friendship.
Norman Vincent Peale

46. The mark of a good action is that it appears inevitable in retrospect.
Robert Louis Stevenson

47. There are risks and costs to a program of action. But they are far less than the long-range risks and costs of comfortable inaction.
John F. Kennedy

48. There comes a moment when you have to stop revving up the car and shove it into gear.
David Mahoney

49. Those who act receive the prizes.
Aristotle

50. When the going gets tough, the tough get going.
Joseph P. Kennedy

Deeds

51.   It is requisite for the relaxation of the mind that we make use,
from time to time, of playful deeds and jokes.
Thomas Aquinas

52.   Our deeds determine us, as much as we determine our deeds.
George Eliot

53.   We live in deeds, not years; in thoughts, not figures on a dial.
We should count time by heart throbs. He most lives who
thinks most, feels the noblest, acts the best.
Philip James Bailey

Doubts

54.   Doubt whom you will, but never doubt yourself.
Christian Nestell Bovee

55.   The only limit to our realization of tomorrow will be our doubts
of today.
Franklin D. Roosevelt

Addiction, alcohol, drugs, denial and habit

Addiction

56.   Every form of addiction is a bad thing, irrespective of whether
it is to alcohol, morphine or idealism.
Carl Gustav Jung

57.   To cease smoking is the easiest thing I ever did. I ought to
know because I've done it a hundred times!
Mark Twain

Alcohol

58.   Alcohol is the anesthesia by which we endure the operation
of life.
George Bernard Shaw

59. Drunkenness is temporary suicide: the happiness that it brings is merely negative, a momentary cessation of unhappiness.
Bertrand Russell

60. First you take a drink, then the drink takes a drink, then the drink takes you.
F. Scott Fitzgerald

61. I like to have a martini,
Two at the very most.
After three I'm under the table,
After four I'm under my host!
Dorothy Parker

62. I'm not a heavy drinker, I can sometimes go for hours without touching a drop.
Noël Coward

63. It provokes the desire, but it takes away the performance. Therefore much drink may be said to be an equivocator with lechery.
William Shakespeare

64. People who drink to drown their sorrow should be told that sorrow knows how to swim.
Ann Landers

65. They who drink beer will think beer.
Washington Irving

66. Yes, madam, I am drunk. But in the morning I will be sober and you will still be ugly.
– *(replying to Lady Astor's comment "Sir, you're drunk!")*
Winston Churchill

Drugs

67. Cocaine is God's way of saying you're making too much money.
Robin Williams

Denial

68. Delay is the deadliest form of denial.
    C. Northcote Parkinson

69. Denial ain't just a river in Egypt.
    Mark Twain

Habit

70. An unfortunate thing about this world is that the good habits are much easier to give up than the bad ones.
    William Somerset Maugham

71. It is easier to prevent bad habits than to break them.
    Benjamin Franklin

72. It is notorious how powerful is the force of habit. The most complex and difficult movements can in time be performed without the least effort or consciousness.
    Charles Darwin

73. Why does a woman work ten years to change a man's habits and then complain that he's not the man she married?
    Barbra Streisand

Adversity and prosperity

74. Comfort and prosperity have never enriched the world as much as adversity has.
    Billy Graham

75. If we had no winter, the spring would not be so pleasant. If we did not sometimes taste of adversity, prosperity would not be so welcome.
    Anne Bradstreet

76. If you can't stand the heat, get out of the kitchen.
    Harry S. Truman

77. Search for the seed of good in every adversity.
    Og Mandino

78. When you come to the end of your rope, tie a knot and hang on.
    Franklin D. Roosevelt

79. When you get into a tight place and everything goes against you, till it seems as though you could not hang on a minute longer, never give up then, for that is just the place and time that the tide will turn.
    Harriet Beecher Stowe

Advice

80. Advice is seldom welcome; and those who want it the most always like it the least.
    Philip Dormer Stanhope

81. Advice is what we ask for when we already know the answer but wish we didn't.
    Erica Jong

82. All of us, at certain moments of our lives, need to take advice and receive help from other people.
    Alexis Carrel

83. Give help rather than advice.
    Marquis De Vauvenargues

84. He that gives good advice, builds with one hand; he that gives good counsel and example, builds with both; but he that gives good admonition and bad example, builds with one hand and pulls down with the other.
    Francis Bacon

85. I always pass on good advice. It is the only thing to do with it. It is never of any use to oneself.
    Oscar Wilde

86. I owe my success to having listened respectfully to the very best advice, and then going away and doing the exact opposite.
G. K. Chesterton

87. The true secret of giving advice is, after you have honestly given it, to be perfectly indifferent whether it is taken or not, and never persist in trying to set people right.
Hannah Whitall Smith

Age and ageing

88. A man ninety years old was asked to what he attributed his longevity. "I reckon," he said, with a twinkle in his eye, "it's because most nights I went to bed and slept when I should have sat up and worried."
Dorothea Kent

89. And in the end, it's not the years in your life that count. It's the life in your years.
Abraham Lincoln

90. By the time you're eighty years old you've learned everything. You only have to remember it.
George Burns

91. From birth to 18 a girl needs good parents. From 18 to 35, she needs good looks. From 35 to 55, good personality. From 55 on, she needs good cash. I'm saving my money.
Sophie Tucker

92. I used to dread getting older because I thought I would not be able to do all the things I wanted to do, but now that I am older I find that I don't want to do them.
Nancy Astor

93. Middle age is when you still believe you'll feel better in the morning.
Bob Hope

94. The man who views the world at 50 the same as he did at 20 has wasted 30 years of his life.
Muhammad Ali

95. The old believe everything; the middle-aged suspect everything; the young know everything.
Oscar Wilde

96. The quality, not the longevity, of one's life is what is important.
Martin Luther King, Jr.

97. You are as young as your faith, as old as your doubt; as young as your self-confidence, as old as your fear; as young as your hope, as old as your despair. In the central place of every heart, there is a recording chamber; so long as it receives messages of beauty, hope, cheer, and courage, so long are you young.
Douglas MacArthur

98. You know you're getting older when the candles cost more than the cake.
Bob Hope

99. Youth is the time of getting, middle age of improving, and old age of spending.
Anne Bradstreet

Ambition

100. Keep away from people who try to belittle your ambitions. Small people always do that, but the really great make you feel that you, too, can become great.
Mark Twain

101. Keep your eyes on the stars, and your feet on the ground.
Theodore Roosevelt

102. No bird soars too high if he soars with his own wings.
William Blake

Appearance, breasts, fashion and style

103. Fashion is the science of appearances, and it inspires one with the desire to seem rather than to be.
Edwin Hubbell Chapin

104. I don't believe makeup and the right hairstyle alone can make a woman beautiful. The most radiant woman in the room is the one full of life and experience.
Sharon Stone

105. I have everything I had twenty years ago—except now it's all lower.
Gypsy Rose Lee

106. I think women see me on the cover of magazines and think I never have a pimple or bags under my eyes. You have to realize that's after two hours of hair and makeup, plus retouching. Even I don't wake up looking like Cindy Crawford.
Cindy Crawford

107. I was the first woman to burn my bra – it took the fire department four days to put it out.
Dolly Parton

108. My husband said "show me your boobs" and I had to pull up my skirt . . . so it was time to get them done!
Dolly Parton

109. Plastic surgeons are always making mountains out of molehills.
Dolly Parton

110. We should look to the mind, and not to the outward appearance.
Aesop

111. You can say what you like about long dresses, but they cover a multitude of shins.
Mae West

112. You'd be surprised how much it costs to look this cheap.
Dolly Parton

Appreciation and approval

113. As much as we thirst for approval we dread condemnation.
    Hans Selye

114. Flattery is from the teeth out. Sincere appreciation is from the heart out.
    Dale Carnegie

115. I became an overachiever to get approval from the world.
    Madonna

116. People who want the most approval get the least and people who need approval the least get the most.
    Wayne Dyer

117. We can secure other people's approval if we do right and try hard; but our own is worth a hundred of it, and no way has been found out of securing that.
    Mark Twain

Arguments, disagreements and compromise

Arguments

118. He knew the precise psychological moment when to say nothing.
    Oscar Wilde

119. He who establishes his argument by noise and command shows that his reason is weak.
    Michel de Montaigne

120. The moment we want to believe something, we suddenly see all the arguments for it, and become blind to the arguments against it.
    George Bernard Shaw

121. The thing I hate about an argument is that it always interrupts a discussion.
    G. K. Chesterton

Disagreements

122. Honest disagreement is often a good sign of progress.
Mahatma Gandhi

Compromise

123. To be or not to be is not a question of compromise. Either you be or you don't be.
Golda Meir

Art, poetry, writers and writing

Art

124. Art is a form of catharsis.
Dorothy Parker

125. Art is a marriage of the conscious and the unconscious.
Jean Cocteau

Poetry

126. A poem records emotions and moods that lie beyond normal language, that can only be patched together and hinted at metaphorically.
Diane Ackerman

127. Poetry is at bottom a criticism of life.
Matthew Arnold

128. Poets don't draw. They unravel their handwriting and then tie it up again, but differently.
Jean Cocteau

Writers and writing

129. The most original thing a writer can do is write like himself. It is also his most difficult task.
Robertson Davies

130. Writing is an adventure. To begin with, it is a toy and an amusement. Then it becomes a mistress, then it becomes a master, then it becomes a tyrant. The last phase is that just as you are about to be reconciled to your servitude, you kill the monster and fling him to the public.
     Winston Churchill

Attitude, beliefs, thinking and thought

Attitude

131. A strong positive mental attitude will create more miracles than any wonder drug.
     Patricia Neal

132. Adopting the right attitude can convert a negative stress into a positive one.
     Hans Selye

133. Attitude is more important than the past, than education, than money, than circumstances, than what people do or say. It is more important than appearance, giftedness, or skill.
     Charles Swindoll

134. Attitudes are more important than facts.
     Karl A. Menninger

135. Could we change our attitude, we should not only see life differently, but life itself would come to be different.
     Katherine Mansfield

136. Human beings, by changing the inner attitudes of their minds, can change the outer aspects of their lives.
     William James

137. It's your aptitude, not just your attitude that determines your ultimate altitude.
     Zig Ziglar

138. One can spend a lifetime assigning blame, finding the cause "out there" for all the troubles that exist. Contrast this with the "responsible attitude" of confronting the situation, bad or good, and instead of asking, "What caused the trouble? Who was to blame?" asking "How can I handle this present situation to make the most of it? What can I salvage here?"
Abraham Maslow

139. Our attitude toward life determines life's attitude towards us.
Earl Nightingale

140. The greatest day in your life and mine is when we take total responsibility for our attitudes. That's the day we truly grow up.
John C. Maxwell

141. The greatest discovery of my generation is that a human being can alter his life by altering his attitudes of mind.
William James

142. The trouble with being number one in the world—in anything—is that it takes a certain mentality to attain that position, and that is something of a driving, perfectionist attitude, so that once you do achieve number one, you don't relax and enjoy it.
Billie Jean King

143. There is little difference in people, but that little difference makes a big difference. That little difference is attitude. The big difference is whether it is positive or negative.
W. Clement Stone

144. We cannot change our past. We cannot change the fact that people act in a certain way. We cannot change the inevitable. The only thing we can do is play on the one string we have, and that is our attitude.
Charles Swindoll

145. We cannot choose how many years we will live, but we can choose how much life those years will have. We cannot control the beauty of our face, but we can control the expression on it. We cannot control life's difficult moments but we can choose to make life less difficult. We cannot control the negative atmosphere of the world, but we can

control the atmosphere of our minds. Too often, we try to
choose and control things we cannot. Too seldom we choose
to control what we can—our attitude.
John C. Maxwell

146.   Words can never adequately convey the incredible impact of
our attitudes toward life. The longer I live the more convinced I
become that life is 10 percent what happens to us and 90
percent how we respond to it.
Charles Swindoll

147.   You cannot control what happens to you, but you can
control your attitude toward what happens to you, and in
that, you will be mastering change rather than allowing it
to master you.
Brian Tracy

Beliefs

148.   Don't limit yourself. Many people limit themselves to what
they think they can do. You can go as far as your mind lets
you. What you believe, you can achieve.
Mary Kay Ash

149.   If you believe you can, you probably can. If you believe you
won't, you most assuredly won't. Belief is the ignition switch
that gets you off the launching pad.
Denis Waitley

150.   People only see what they are prepared to see.
Ralph Waldo Emerson

151.   You have to believe in yourself, that's the secret. Even when I
was in the orphanage, when I was roaming the street trying to
find enough to eat, even then I thought of myself as the
greatest actor in the world.
Charlie Chaplin

Thinking and thought

152.   Change your thoughts, and you change your world.
Norman Vincent Peale

153. "Doublethink" means the power of holding two contradictory beliefs in one's mind simultaneously, and accepting both of them.
George Orwell

154. It is the mark of an educated mind to be able to entertain a thought without accepting it.
Aristotle

155. Most people would rather die than think; in fact, they do so.
Bertrand Russell

156. The "how" thinker gets problems solved effectively because he wastes no time with futile "ifs".
Norman Vincent Peale

157. The happiness of your life depends on the quality of your thoughts.
Marcus Aurelius Antoninus

158. The highest possible stage in moral culture is when we recognize that we ought to control our thoughts.
Charles Darwin

159. The human mind prefers to be spoon-fed with the thoughts of others, but deprived of such nourishment it will, reluctantly, begin to think for itself—and such thinking, remember, is original thinking and may have valuable results.
Agatha Christie

160. Thinking is the hardest work there is, which is the probable reason why so few engage in it.
Henry Ford

161. Thought is action in rehearsal.
Sigmund Freud

162. Thought is the blossom; language the bud; action the fruit behind it.
Ralph Waldo Emerson

B

Beauty

163. As we grow old, the beauty steals inward.
    Ralph Waldo Emerson

164. Beauty is a radiance that originates from within and comes
    from inner security and strong character.
    Jane Seymour

165. Beauty is not quality in things themselves: It exists merely in
    the mind which contemplates them; and each mind perceives a
    different beauty.
    David Hume

166. Everything has its beauty but not everyone sees it.
    Confucius

167. I slept, and dreamed that life was Beauty;
    I woke, and found that life was Duty.
    Ellen Sturgis Hooper

168. The best and most beautiful things in the world cannot be
    seen or even touched. They must be felt with the heart.
    Helen Keller

169. The soul that sees beauty may sometimes walk alone.
    Johann Wolfgang von Goethe

170. Though we travel the world over to find the beautiful, we must
    carry it with us or we find it not.
    Ralph Waldo Emerson

171. When beauty fires the blood, how love exalts the mind.
    John Dryden

Books and diaries

Books

172. A book is a garden, an orchard, a storehouse, a party, a
      company by the way, a counselor, a multitude of counselors.
      Henry Ward Beecher

173. Never lend books, for no one ever returns them. The only books
      I have in my library are those that other folks have lent me.
      Anatole France

Diaries

174. It's the good girls who keep the diaries; the bad girls never
      have the time.
      Tallulah Bankhead

175. Painting is just another way of keeping a diary.
      Pablo Picasso

C

Change

176. All changes, even the most longed for, have their melancholy; for what we leave behind is a part of ourselves; we must die to one life before we can enter into another!
Gail Sheehy

177. Change can either challenge or threaten us. Your beliefs pave your way to success or block you.
Marsha Sinetar

178. Consider how hard it is to change yourself and you'll understand what little chance you have in trying to change others.
Jacob M. Braude

179. I've continued to recognize the power individuals have to change virtually anything and everything in their lives in an instant. I've learned that the resources we need to turn our dreams into reality are within us, merely waiting for the day when we decide to wake up and claim our birthright.
Anthony Robbins

180. There is a certain relief in change, even though it be from bad to worse! As I have often found in travelling in a stagecoach, that it is often a comfort to shift one's position, and be bruised in a new place.
Washington Irving

181. To exist is to change, to change is to mature, to mature is to go on creating oneself endlessly.
Henri Bergson

182. We are taught you must blame your father, your sisters, your brothers, the school, the teachers—but never blame yourself. It's never your fault. But it's always your fault, because if you wanted to change you're the one who has got to change.
Katharine Hepburn

183. You don't have to be the Dalai Lama to tell people that life's about change.
John Cleese

184. You must be the change you wish to see in the world.
Mahatma Gandhi

185. You must take personal responsibility. You cannot change the circumstances, the seasons, or the wind, but you can change yourself. That is something you have charge of.
Jim Rohn

186. Your life changes the moment you make a new, congruent, and committed decision.
Anthony Robbins

Chaos and order

Chaos

187. Chaos is a name for any order that produces confusion in our minds.
George Santayana

188. Chaos often breeds life, when order breeds habit.
Henry Brooks Adams

189. Freedom is just chaos, with better lighting.
Alan Dean Foster

Order

190. Cleanliness and order are not matters of instinct; they are matters of education, and like most great things, you must cultivate a taste for them.
Benjamin Disraeli

191. To put the world in order, we must first put the nation in order; to put the nation in order, we must put the family in order; to put the family in order, we must cultivate our personal life; and to cultivate our personal life, we must first set our hearts right.
Confucius

Character and personality

Character

192. A man's character is the reality of himself; his reputation, the opinion others have formed about him; character resides in him, reputation in other people; that is the substance, this is the shadow.
Henry Ward Beecher

193. Be more concerned with your character than your reputation. Your character is what you really are while your reputation is merely what others think you are.
John Wooden

194. By constant self-discipline and self-control you can develop greatness of character.
Grenville Kleiser

195. Character building begins in our infancy, and continues until death.
Eleanor Roosevelt

196. Character cannot be developed in ease and quiet. Only through experience of trial and suffering can the soul be strengthened, ambition inspired, and success achieved.
Helen Keller

197. Character is a by-product; it is produced in the great manufacture of daily duty.
Woodrow Wilson

198. Character is like a tree and reputation like its shadow. The shadow is what we think of it; the tree is the real thing.
Abraham Lincoln

199. Conscience is the frame of character, and love is the covering for it.
Henry Ward Beecher

200. Every man has three characters—that which he exhibits, that which he has, and that which he thinks he has.
Alphonse Karr

201. Sound character provides the power with which a person may ride the emergencies of life instead of being overwhelmed by them.
    Og Mandino

202. Study carefully, the character of the one you recommend, lest their misconduct bring you shame.
    Marcus Tullius Cicero

Personality

203. I recognise that I am made up of several persons
    and that the person that at the moment has the upper hand
    will inevitably give place to another.
    But which is the real one?
    All of them or none?
    William Somerset Maugham

204. The meeting of two personalities is like the contact of two chemical substances: if there is any reaction, both are transformed.
    Carl Gustav Jung

Commitment and enthusiasm

Commitment

205. I believe life is constantly testing us for our level of commitment, and life's greatest rewards are reserved for those who demonstrate a never-ending commitment to act until they achieve. This level of resolve can move mountains, but it must be constant and consistent. As simplistic as this may sound, it is still the common denominator separating those who live their dreams from those who live in regret.
    Anthony Robbins

Enthusiasm

206. If passion drives you, let reason hold the reins.
    Benjamin Franklin

207.   Nothing great was ever achieved without enthusiasm.
Ralph Waldo Emerson

208.   There is a real magic in enthusiasm. It spells the difference between mediocrity and accomplishment.
Norman Vincent Peale

209.   We act as though comfort and luxury were the chief requirements of life, when all that we need to make us really happy is something to be enthusiastic about.
Charles Kingsley

210.   You can do anything if you have enthusiasm. Enthusiasm is the yeast that makes your hopes rise to the stars. With it, there is accomplishment. Without it there are only alibis.
Henry Ford

Communication, listening, talking and words

Communication: verbal and non-verbal

211.   Good communication is as stimulating as black coffee and just as hard to sleep after.
Anne Morrow Lindbergh

212.   It is only the women whose eyes have been washed clear with tears who get the broad vision that makes them little sisters to all the world.
Dorothy Dix

213.   Take advantage of every opportunity to practice your communication skills so that when important occasions arise, you will have the gift, the style, the sharpness, the clarity, and the emotions to affect other people.
Jim Rohn

214.   Tears are the noble language of the eye.
Robert Herrick

215.   Tears at times have all the weight of speech.
Ovid

216. The most important thing in communication is to hear what isn't being said.
Peter Drucker

217. There is a sacredness in tears. They are not the mark of weakness, but of power. They speak more eloquently than ten thousand tongues. They are messengers of overwhelming grief . . . and unspeakable love.
Washington Irving

218. To effectively communicate, we must realize that we are all different in the way we perceive the world and use this understanding as a guide to our communication with others.
Anthony Robbins

219. When the eyes say one thing and the tongue another, the practiced person relies on the language of the first.
Ralph Waldo Emerson

220. Years ago, I tried to top everybody, but I don't anymore. I realized it was killing conversation. When you're always trying for a topper you aren't really listening. It ruins communication.
Groucho Marx

Listening

221. Good listening is the key to skilful communication. It is one of the most priceless gifts we can offer other people. When a person feels listened to they feel accepted, valued, respected, heard and understood.
Jan Sutton

222. I like to listen. I have learned a great deal from listening carefully. Most people never listen.
Ernest Hemingway

223. It is the province of knowledge to speak and it is the privilege of wisdom to listen.
Oliver Wendell Holmes

224. Know how to listen, and you will profit even from those who talk badly.
Plutarch

225. Listen long enough and the person will generally come up with an adequate solution.
Mary Kay Ash

226. Listening is a magnetic and strange thing, a creative force. The friends who listen to us are the ones we move toward. When we are listened to, it creates us, makes us unfold and expand.
Karl A. Menninger

227. So when you are listening to somebody, completely, attentively, then you are listening not only to the words, but also to the feeling of what is being conveyed, to the whole of it, not part of it.
Jiddu Krishnamurti

228. To listen closely and reply well is the highest perfection we are able to attain in the art of conversation.
François La Rochefoucauld

229. When you listen with empathy to another person, you give that person psychological air.
Stephen R. Covey

230. You cannot truly listen to anyone and do anything else at the same time.
M. Scott Peck

Talking

231. For God's sake, don't say yes until I've finished talking.
Darryl F. Zanuck

232. I don't mind how much my ministers talk—as long as they do what I say.
Margaret Thatcher

233. I must indeed, try hard to control the talking habit, but I'm afraid that little can be done, as my case is hereditary. My mother, too, is fond of chatting, and has handed this weakness down to me.
Anne Frank

234. One never realizes how much and how little he knows until he starts talking.
     Louis L'Amour

235. She did not talk to people as if they were strange hard shells she had to crack open to get inside. She talked as if she were already in the shell. In their very shell.
     Marita Bonner

236. Talking much is a sign of vanity, for the one who is lavish with words is cheap in deeds.
     Sir Walter Raleigh

Words

237. A torn jacket is soon mended; but hard words bruise the heart of a child.
     Henry Wadsworth Longfellow

238. Kind words can be short and easy to speak, but their echoes are truly endless.
     Mother Teresa

239. Short words are best and the old words when short are best of all.
     Winston Churchill

240. The most valuable of all talents is that of never using two words when one will do.
     Thomas Jefferson

241. Words are loaded pistols.
     Jean-Paul Sartre

242. Words are, of course, the most powerful drug used by mankind.
     Rudyard Kipling

243. Words do two major things: They provide food for the mind and create light for understanding and awareness.
     Jim Rohn

244.   Words may be false and full of art;
       Sighs are the natural language of the heart.
       Thomas Shadwell

245.   Words mean more than what is set down on paper. It takes the
       human voice to infuse them with shades of deeper meaning.
       Maya Angelou

Compliments, encouragement and praise

Compliments

246.   Being taken for granted can be a compliment. It means that
       you've become a comfortable, trusted person in another
       person's life.
       Dr. Joyce Brothers

247.   I can live for two months on a good compliment.
       Mark Twain

Encouragement

248.   Flatter me, and I may not believe you. Criticize me, and I may
       not like you. Ignore me, and I may not forgive you. Encourage
       me, and I will not forget you.
       William Arthur Ward

249.   Surround yourself with only people who are going to lift you
       higher.
       Oprah Winfrey

Praise

250.   Get someone else to blow your horn and the sound will carry
       twice as far.
       Will Rogers

251.   Praise invariably implies a reference to a higher standard.
       Aristotle

252. The more credit you give away, the more will come back to you. The more you help others, the more they will want to help you.
Brian Tracy

Confession and truth

Confession

253. It is confession, not the priest, that gives us absolution.
Oscar Wilde

254. We must confess that we have broken God's Laws, and we must be willing to renounce our sins. This is the first step to happiness, peace and contentment.
Billy Graham

Truth

255. If one tells the truth, one is sure, sooner or later, to be found out.
Oscar Wilde

256. It is always the best policy to speak the truth, unless of course you are an exceptionally good liar.
Jerome K. Jerome

257. Tell the truth and shame the devil.
François Rabelais

258. The most exhausting thing in life, I have discovered, is being insincere.
Anne Morrow Lindbergh

259. To be natural is such a very difficult pose to keep up.
Oscar Wilde

Conflict and confrontation

Conflict

260. The most intense conflicts, if overcome, leave behind a sense of security and calm that is not easily disturbed. It is just these intense conflicts and their conflagration which are needed to produce valuable and lasting results.
   Carl Gustav Jung

Confrontation

261. To confront a person with his own shadow is to show him his own light.
   Carl Gustav Jung

Conscience

262. An individual who breaks a law that conscience tells him is unjust, and who willingly accepts the penalty of imprisonment in order to arouse the conscience of the community over its injustice, is in reality expressing the highest respect for the law.
   Martin Luther King, Jr.

Courage, determination, perseverance, persistence and willpower

Courage

263. Courage is the first of human qualities because it is the quality which guarantees the others.
   Aristotle

264. Courage is very important. Like a muscle, it is strengthened by use.
   Ruth Gordon

265. Life is mostly froth and bubble;
     Two things stand like stone,
     Kindness is another's trouble,
     Courage is your own.
     Adam Lindsay Gordon

266. The mighty oak was once a little nut that stood its ground.
     Anon.

Determination

267. Determination is the wake-up call to the human will.
     Anthony Robbins

268. Just don't give up trying to do what you really want to
     do. Where there's love and inspiration, I don't think you can
     go wrong.
     Ella Fitzgerald

269. You may have to fight a battle more than once to win it.
     Margaret Thatcher

Perseverance

270. By perseverance the snail reached the ark.
     Charles Spurgeon

271. Great works are performed not by strength, but by
     perseverance.
     Samuel Johnson

272. Perseverance is failing nineteen times and succeeding the
     twentieth.
     Julie Andrews

273. The difference between perseverance and obstinacy is, that
     one often comes from a strong will, and the other from a
     strong won't.
     Henry Ward Beecher

Persistence

274. That which we persist in doing becomes easier for us to do;
      not that the nature of the thing itself is changed, but that our
      power to do is increased.
      Ralph Waldo Emerson

Willpower

275. Willpower is only the tensile strength of one's own disposition.
      One cannot increase it by a single ounce.
      Cesare Pavese

Creating a crisis

276. Some people have such a talent for making the best of a bad
      situation that they go around creating bad situations so they
      can make the best of them.
      Jean Kerr

Creativity and curiosity

Creativity

277. Creativity comes from trust. Trust your instincts. And never
      hope more than you work.
      Rita Mae Brown

278. The creative individual is particularly gifted in seeing the gap
      between what is and what could be (which means, of course,
      that he has achieved a certain measure of detachment from
      what is).
      John W. Gardner

Curiosity

279. Curiosity is the wick in the candle of learning.
      William Arthur Ward

280. I could not, at any age, be content to take my place by the fireside and simply look on. Life was meant to be lived and curiosity must be kept alive. One must never, for whatever reason, turn his back on life.
Eleanor Roosevelt

281. I think, at a child's birth, if a mother could ask a fairy godmother to endow it with the most useful gift, that gift would be curiosity.
Eleanor Roosevelt

282. We keep moving forward, opening new doors, and doing new things, because we're curious and curiosity keeps leading us down new paths.
Walt Disney

Criticism, feedback, judgement, prejudice and sarcasm

Criticism

283. Criticism is prejudice made plausible.
H. L. Mencken

284. Criticism, as it was first instituted by Aristotle, was meant as a standard of judging well.
Samuel Johnson

285. Criticize the act, not the person.
Mary Kay Ash

286. Do what you feel in your heart to be right, for you'll be criticized anyway. You'll be damned if you do and damned if you don't.
Eleanor Roosevelt

287. I love criticism just so long as it's unqualified praise.
Noël Coward

288. If you are not being criticized, you may not be doing much.
Donald Rumsfeld

289. Sandwich every bit of criticism between two layers of praise.
     Mary Kay Ash

290. The trouble with most of us is that we would rather be ruined by praise than saved by criticism.
     Norman Vincent Peale

291. To escape criticism—do nothing, say nothing, be nothing.
     Elbert Hubbard

292. Whenever you have truth it must be given with love, or the message and the messenger will be rejected.
     Mahatma Gandhi

Feedback

293. Feedback is the breakfast of champions.
     Kenneth Blanchard

Judgement

294. I went for years not finishing anything. Because, of course, when you finish something you can be judged . . . I had poems which were re-written so many times I suspect it was just a way of avoiding sending them out.
     Erica Jong

295. If you judge people, you have no time to love them.
     Mother Teresa

296. One cool judgment is worth a thousand hasty counsels. The thing to do is to supply light and not heat.
     Woodrow Wilson

Prejudice

297. I have a dream that my four little children will one day live in a nation where they will not be judged by the color of their skin but by the content of their character.
     Martin Luther King, Jr.

298. I'm interested in the fact that the less secure a man is, the more likely he is to have extreme prejudice.
Clint Eastwood

299. Prejudice comes from being in the dark; sunlight disinfects it.
Muhammad Ali

300. Prejudices, it is well known, are most difficult to eradicate from the heart whose soil has never been loosened or fertilized by education; they grow there, firm as weeds among stones.
Charlotte Brontë

301. The mind of a bigot is like the pupil of the eye; the more light you pour on it, the more it will contract.
Oliver Wendell Holmes

Sarcasm

302. Sarcasm I now see to be, in general, the language of the devil; for which reason I have long since as good as renounced it.
Thomas Carlyle

D

Diet, gluttony and weight

Diet

303. I feel about airplanes the way I feel about diets. It seems to me that they are wonderful things for other people to go on.
Jean Kerr

Gluttony

304. Gluttony is an emotional escape, a sign something is eating us.
Peter De Vries

305. I am not a glutton—I am an explorer of food.
Erma Bombeck

Weight

306. I found there was only one way to look thin—hang out with fat people.
Rodney Dangerfield

307. To ask women to become unnaturally thin is to ask them to relinquish their sexuality.
Naomi Wolf

Dignity

308. Never bend your head. Always hold it high. Look the world right in the eye.
Helen Keller

Dreams and destiny

Dreams

309. It takes a lot of courage to show your dreams to someone else.
Erma Bombeck

310. Since it doesn't cost a dime to dream, you'll never shortchange yourself when you stretch your imagination.
Robert Schuller

311. Some people see things as they are and say why. I dream things that never were and say why not?
Robert F. Kennedy

Destiny

312. It is a mistake to look too far ahead. Only one link in the chain of destiny can be handled at a time.
Winston Churchill

313. It's not what's happening to you now or what has happened in your past that determines who you become. Rather, it's your decisions about what to focus on, what things mean to you, and what you're going to do about them that will determine your ultimate destiny.
Anthony Robbins

Education, learning and teaching

Education

314. An education isn't how much you have committed to memory, or even how much you know. It's being able to differentiate between what you do know and what you don't.
Anatole France

315. Education is the best provision for old age.
Aristotle

316. When the student is ready, the master appears.
Buddhist Proverb

317. While formal schooling is an important advantage, it is not a guarantee of success nor is its absence a fatal handicap.
Ray Kroc

Learning

318. I have learned silence from the talkative, toleration from the intolerant, and kindness from the unkind; yet strange, I am ungrateful to those teachers.
Kahlil Gibran

319. Never become so much of an expert that you stop gaining expertise. View life as a continuous learning experience.
Denis Waitley

Teaching

320. A master can tell you what he expects of you. A teacher, though awakens your own expectations.
Patricia Neal

321. A teacher affects eternity; he can never tell where his influence stops.
Henry Brooks Adams

322. I cannot teach anybody anything, I can only make them think.
Socrates

323. If you give me rice, I'll eat today;
if you teach me how to grow rice, I'll eat every day.
Mahatma Gandhi

324. The mediocre teacher tells. The good teacher explains. The superior teacher demonstrates. The great teacher inspires.
William Arthur Ward

Epitaph

325. Here lies a poor woman who always was tired,
For she lived in a place where help wasn't hired.
Her last words on earth were, Dear friends I am going
Where washing ain't done nor sweeping nor sewing
And everything there is exact to my wishes
For there they don't eat and there's no washing of dishes.
Don't mourn for me now, don't mourn for me never
For I'm going to do nothing for ever and ever.
Anon.

Equality

326. Equality consists in the same treatment of similar persons.
Aristotle

327. Equality may perhaps be a right, but no power on earth can ever turn it into a fact.
Honoré de Balzac

328. Everybody should have an equal chance—but they shouldn't have a flying start.
Harold Wilson

329. Instead of getting hard ourselves and trying to compete,
     women should try to give their best qualities to men—bring
     them softness, teach them how to cry.
     Joan Baez

330. Some will always be above others. Destroy the inequality
     today, and it will appear again tomorrow.
     Ralph Waldo Emerson

331. Women's battle for financial equality has barely been joined,
     much less won. Society still traditionally assigns to woman the
     role of money-handler rather than money-maker, and our
     assigned specialty is far more likely to be home economics
     than financial economics.
     Paula Nelson

Experience

332. Experience is a good teacher, but she sends in terrific bills.
     Minna Thomas Antrim

333. Experience is the name we give to our mistakes.
     Oscar Wilde

Eyes

334. An eye can threaten like a loaded and levelled gun, or it can
     insult like hissing or kicking; or, in its altered mood, by beams
     of kindness, it can make the heart dance for joy.
     Ralph Waldo Emerson

335. He who can no longer pause to wonder and stand rapt in awe;
     is as good as dead; his eyes are closed.
     Albert Einstein

336. Her eyes are homes of silent prayer.
     Alfred Lord Tennyson

337. I look in the mirror through the eyes of the child that was me.
     Judy Collins

338. It needs no dictionary of quotations to remind me that the
     eyes are the windows of the soul.
     Max Beerbohm

339. The eye sees only what the mind is prepared to comprehend.
     Robertson Davies

340. The soul, fortunately, has an interpreter—often an unconscious,
     but still a truthful interpreter—in the eye.
     Charlotte Brontë

F

Faults and mistakes

Faults

341. Don't find fault, find a remedy.
Henry Ford

342. None of us can stand other people having the same faults as ourselves.
Oscar Wilde

Mistakes

343. From error to error one discovers the entire truth.
Sigmund Freud

344. If you simply take up the attitude of defending a mistake, there will no hope of improvement.
Winston Churchill

345. If you're not making mistakes, then you're not doing anything. I'm positive that a doer makes mistakes.
John Wooden

346. It isn't making mistakes that's critical; it's correcting them and getting on with the principal task.
Donald Rumsfeld

347. Mistakes are painful when they happen, but years later a collection of mistakes is what is called experience.
Denis Waitley

348. Show me a person who has never made a mistake and I'll show you somebody who has never achieved much.
Joan Collins

349. There are no mistakes, no coincidences, all events are blessings given to us to learn from.
Elisabeth Kübler-Ross

350. To make mistakes is human; to stumble is commonplace; to be able to laugh at yourself is maturity.
William Arthur Ward

Feelings and emotions

Feelings and emotions – general

351. Find expression for a sorrow, and it will become dear to you. Find an expression for joy, and you will intensify its ecstasy.
Oscar Wilde

352. I can see the humorous side of things and enjoy the fun when it comes; but look where I will, there seems to me always more sadness than joy in life.
Jerome K. Jerome

353. I don't know what other singers feel when they articulate lyrics, but being an 18-karat manic-depressive and having lived a life of violent emotional contradictions, I have an over acute capacity for sadness as well as elation. I know what the cat who wrote the song is trying to say. I've been there—and back. I guess the audience feels it along with me. They can't help it. Sentimentality, after all, is an emotion common to all humanity.
Frank Sinatra

354. I wear my heart on my sleeve.
Princess Diana

355. I wish thar was winders to my Sole, sed I,
so that you could see some of my feelins.
Artemus Ward

356. If I feel depressed I will sing. If I feel sad I will laugh. If I feel ill I will double my labor. If I feel fear I will plunge ahead. If I feel inferior I will wear new garments. If I feel uncertain I will raise my voice.
Og Mandino

357.   If one lets fear or hate or anger take possession of the mind, they become self-forged chains.
Helen Gahagan Douglas

358.   Intense feeling too often obscures the truth.
Harry S. Truman

359.   The degree of one's emotion varies inversely with one's knowledge of the facts—the less you know the hotter you get.
Bertrand Russell

360.   There can be no transforming of darkness into light and of apathy into movement without emotion.
Carl Gustav Jung

361.   To wear your heart on your sleeve isn't a very good plan; you should wear it inside, where it functions best.
Margaret Thatcher

Feelings and emotions – specific

Agony

362.   There is no agony like bearing an untold story inside of you.
Maya Angelou

Anger

363.   A sharp tongue is the only edge tool that grows keener with constant use.
Washington Irving

364.   Anger and intolerance are the twin enemies of correct understanding.
Mahatma Gandhi

365.   Anger begins with folly, and ends with repentance.
Beverly Sills

366.   Anger is a symptom, a way of cloaking and expressing feelings too awful to experience directly—hurt, bitterness, grief and, most of all, fear.
Joan Rivers

367.   Because society would rather we always wore a pretty face,
       women have been trained to cut off anger.
       Nancy Friday

368.   Don't hold to anger, hurt or pain. They steal your energy and
       keep you from love.
       Leo Buscaglia

369.   For every minute you are angry you lose sixty seconds of
       happiness.
       Ralph Waldo Emerson

370.   Get mad, then get over it.
       Colin Powell

371.   Holding on to anger is like grasping a hot coal with the intent
       of throwing it at someone else; you are the one getting burned.
       Buddha

372.   I was angry with my friend:
       I told my wrath, my wrath did end.
       I was angry with my foe:
       I told it not, my wrath did grow.
       William Blake

373.   If you do not wish to be prone to anger, do not feed the habit;
       give it nothing which may tend to its increase.
       Epictetus

374.   In a controversy the instant we feel anger we have already
       ceased striving for the truth, and have begun striving for
       ourselves.
       Thomas Carlyle

375.   It is wise to direct your anger towards problems—not people; to
       focus your energies on answers—not excuses.
       William Arthur Ward

376.   It takes two flints to make a fire.
       Louisa May Alcott

377.   That old law about "an eye for an eye" leaves everybody blind.
       The time is always right to do the right thing.
       Martin Luther King, Jr.

378. The man who gets angry at the right things and with the right people, and in the right way and at the right time and for the right length of time, is commended.
Aristotle

379. The more anger towards the past you carry in your heart, the less capable you are of loving in the present.
Barbara De Angelis

380. We boil at different degrees.
Ralph Waldo Emerson

381. Whatever is begun in anger, ends in shame.
Benjamin Franklin

382. When anger rises, think of the consequences.
Confucius

383. You can't shake hands with a clenched fist.
Indira Gandhi

Anticipation

384. Do not anticipate trouble, or worry about what may never happen. Keep in the sunlight.
Benjamin Franklin

385. Nothing is so good as it seems beforehand.
George Eliot

386. What we anticipate seldom occurs; what we least expected generally happens.
Benjamin Disraeli

Bitterness

387. Bitterness imprisons life; love releases it. Bitterness paralyzes life; love empowers it. Bitterness sours life; love sweetens it. Bitterness sickens life; love heals it. Bitterness blinds life; love anoints its eyes.
Harry Emerson Fosdick

Boredom

388. Boredom is the feeling that everything is a waste of time; serenity, that nothing is.
Thomas Szasz

Contempt

389. Between flattery and admiration there often flows a river of contempt.
Minna Thomas Antrim

Envy

390. Envy always implies conscious inferiority wherever it resides.
Pliny the Elder

391. Fools may our scorn, not envy, raise, for envy is a kind of praise.
John Gay

392. The few who do are the envy of the many who only watch.
Jim Rohn

Fear

393. Do the thing you fear and the death of fear is certain.
Ralph Waldo Emerson

394. Fear imprisons, faith liberates; fear paralyzes, faith empowers; fear disheartens, faith encourages; fear sickens, faith heals; fear makes useless, faith makes serviceable.
Harry Emerson Fosdick

395. Fear is an emotion indispensable for survival.
Hannah Arendt

396. I fear waking up one morning and finding out it was all for nothing. We're here for a reason. I believe a bit of the reason is to throw little torches out to lead people through the dark.
Whoopi Goldberg

397. I have accepted fear as a part of life—specifically the fear of change. . . . I have gone ahead despite the pounding in the heart that says: turn back!
Erica Jong

398. No passion so effectively robs the mind of all its powers of acting and reasoning as fear.
Edmund Burke

399. Our deepest fear is not that we are inadequate. Our deepest fear is that we are powerful beyond measure. It is our light, not our darkness, that most frightens us.
Nelson Mandela

400. The fear of being laughed at makes cowards of us all.
Mignon McLaughlin

401. To a man who is afraid everything rustles.
Sophocles

402. We are more often frightened than hurt; and we suffer more from imagination than from reality.
Seneca

403. We pay a heavy price for our fear of failure. It is a powerful obstacle to growth. It assures the progressive narrowing of the personality and prevents exploration and experimentation. There is no learning without some difficulty and fumbling. If you want to keep on learning, you must keep on risking failure—all your life.
John W. Gardner

404. What is needed, rather than running away or controlling or suppressing or any other resistance, is understanding fear; that means, watch it, learn about it, come directly into contact with it. We are to learn about fear, not how to escape from it.
Jiddu Krishnamurti

405. You cease to be afraid when you cease to hope;
for hope is accompanied by fear.
Seneca

Forgiveness

406. "I can forgive, but I cannot forget," is only another way of saying, "I cannot forgive."
Henry Ward Beecher

407. Confront the dark parts of yourself, and work to banish them with illumination and forgiveness. Your willingness to wrestle with your demons will cause your angels to sing. Use the pain as fuel, as a reminder of your strength.
August Wilson

408. If you haven't forgiven yourself something, how can you forgive others?
Dolores Huerta

Grief and loss

409. Grief knits two hearts in closer bonds than happiness ever can; and common sufferings are far stronger links than common joys.
Alphonse De Lamartine

410. Nothing that grieves us can be called little: by the eternal laws of proportion a child's loss of a doll and a king's loss of a crown are events of the same size.
Mark Twain

411. The greatest griefs are those we cause ourselves.
Sophocles

412. To spare oneself from grief at all costs can be achieved only at the price of total detachment, which excludes the ability to experience happiness.
Erich Fromm

413. We never understand how little we need in this world until we know the loss of it.
James Matthew Barrie

414. While grief is fresh, every attempt to divert only irritates. You must wait till grief be digested, and then amusement will dissipate the remains of it.
Samuel Johnson

Guilt

415. Each snowflake in an avalanche pleads not guilty.
      Stanislaw J. Lec

416. From the body of one guilty deed a thousand ghostly fears and
      haunting thoughts proceed.
      William Wordsworth

417. Guilt: the gift that keeps on giving.
      Erma Bombeck

Happiness

418. For happiness one needs security, but joy can spring like a
      flower even from the cliffs of despair.
      Anne Morrow Lindbergh

419. Happiness is not something you postpone for the future; it is
      something you design for the present.
      Jim Rohn

420. Many persons have the wrong idea of what constitutes true
      happiness. It is not attained through self-gratification but
      through fidelity to a worthy purpose.
      Helen Keller

421. The secret of happiness is this: let your interests be as wide as
      possible, and let your reactions to the things and persons that
      interest you be as far as possible friendly rather than hostile.
      Bertrand Russell

422. True happiness arises, in the first place, from the enjoyment of
      one's self, and in the next, from the friendship and
      conversation of a few select companions.
      Joseph Addison

Hate

423. A man's hatred is always concentrated upon that which makes
      him conscious of his bad qualities.
      Carl Gustav Jung

424. Hating people because of their color is wrong. And it doesn't matter which color does the hating. It's just plain wrong.
Muhammad Ali

425. Hatred paralyzes life; love releases it. Hatred confuses life; love harmonizes it. Hatred darkens life; love illuminates it.
Martin Luther King, Jr.

426. I imagine one of the reasons people cling to their hates so stubbornly is because they sense, once hate is gone, they will be forced to deal with pain.
James Baldwin

Hope

427. Hope is both the earliest and the most indispensable virtue inherent in the state of being alive. If life is to be sustained hope must remain, even where confidence is wounded, trust impaired.
Erik Erikson

428. My hopes are not always realized, but I always hope.
Ovid

429. Practice hope. As hopefulness becomes a habit, you can achieve a permanently happy spirit.
Norman Vincent Peale

Inferiority

430. No one can make you feel inferior without your consent.
Eleanor Roosevelt

431. The greater the feeling of inferiority that has been experienced, the more powerful is the urge to conquest and the more violent the emotional agitation.
Alfred Adler

Jealousy

432. Jealousy is all the fun you think they had.
Erica Jong

433.   More men die of jealousy than of cancer.
       Joseph P. Kennedy

434.   To jealousy, nothing is more frightful than laughter.
       Françoise Sagan

Loneliness

435.   If I'm such a legend, then why am I so lonely? Let me tell you, legends are all very well if you've got somebody around who loves you.
       Judy Garland

436.   Loneliness and the feeling of being unwanted is the most terrible poverty.
       Mother Teresa

437.   Nothing makes us so lonely as our secrets.
       Paul Tournier

438.   The loneliness you get by the sea is personal and alive. It doesn't subdue you and make you feel abject. It's stimulating loneliness.
       Anne Morrow Lindbergh

439.   The whole conviction of my life now rests upon the belief that loneliness, far from being a rare and curious phenomenon, peculiar to myself and to a few other solitary men, is the central and inevitable fact of human existence.
       Thomas Wolfe

440.   You cannot be lonely if you like the person you're alone with.
       Wayne Dyer

Pride

441.   Pride is a tricky, glorious, double-edged feeling.
       Adrienne Rich

442.   Pride that dines on vanity, sups on contempt.
       Benjamin Franklin

Revenge

443.   A man that studieth revenge keeps his own wounds green,
which otherwise would heal and do well.
Francis Bacon

Sadness

444.   The walls we build around us to keep sadness out also keep
out the joy.
Jim Rohn

Shame and humiliation

445.   The basis of shame is not some personal mistake of ours, but
the ignominy, the humiliation we feel that we must be what
we are without any choice in the matter, and that this
humiliation is seen by everyone.
Milan Kundera

446.   The most important thing is to be whatever you are without
shame.
Rod Steiger

Football

447.   He dribbles a lot and the opposition don't like it—you can see
it all over their faces.
Ron Atkinson

448.   If a man watches three football games in a row, he should be
declared legally dead.
Erma Bombeck

449.   Some people believe football is a matter of life and death. I
am very disappointed with that attitude. I can assure you it is
much, much more important than that.
Bill Shankly

G

Giving and helping others

Giving

450. From what we get, we can make a living; what we give, however, makes a life.
Arthur Ashe

451. To give real service you must add something which cannot be bought or measured with money, and that is sincerity and integrity.
Douglas Adams

452. To give without any reward, or any notice, has a special quality of its own.
Anne Morrow Lindbergh

453. You give but little when you give of your possessions. It is when you give of yourself that you truly give.
Kahlil Gibran

Helping others

454. As you grow older you will discover that you have two hands. One for helping yourself, the other for helping others.
Audrey Hepburn

455. Do something for somebody every day for which you do not get paid.
Albert Schweitzer

456. If you haven't any charity in your heart, you have the worst kind of heart trouble.
Bob Hope

457. Only a life lived for others is the life worth while.
Albert Einstein

458.   Too often we underestimate the power of a touch, a smile, a
       kind word, a listening ear, an honest compliment, or the
       smallest act of caring, all of which have the potential to turn a
       life around.
       Leo Buscaglia

459.   We make a living by what we get. We make a life by what we
       give.
       Winston Churchill

Goals, obstacles, decisions and solutions

Goals

460.   A goal is a dream with a deadline.
       Napoleon Hill

461.   A good goal is like a strenuous exercise—it makes you stretch.
       Mary Kay Ash

462.   First, have a definite, clear, practical ideal: a goal, an objective.
       Second, have the necessary means to achieve your ends:
       wisdom, money, materials and methods. Third, adjust all your
       means to that end.
       Aristotle

463.   Goals are a means to an end, not the ultimate purpose of our
       lives. They are simply a tool to concentrate our focus and move
       us in a direction. The only reason we really pursue goals is to
       cause ourselves to expand and grow. Achieving goals by
       themselves will never make us happy in the long term; it's who
       you become, as you overcome the obstacles necessary to
       achieve your goals, that can give you the deepest and most
       long-lasting sense of fulfillment.
       Anthony Robbins

464.   Goals provide the energy source that powers our lives. One of the
       best ways we can get the most from the energy we have is to
       focus it. That is what goals can do for us; concentrate our energy.
       Denis Waitley

465. Hitch your wagon to a star.
      Ralph Waldo Emerson

466. If you're climbing the ladder of life, you go rung by rung, one
      step at a time. Don't look too far up, set your goals high but take
      one step at a time. Sometimes you don't think you're progressing
      until you step back and see how high you've really gone.
      Donny Osmond

467. To live only for some future goal is shallow. It's the sides of the
      mountain that sustain life, not the top.
      Robert M. Pirsig

Obstacles

468. Obstacles are those frightful things you see when you take
      your eyes off your goal.
      Henry Ford

469. Stand up to your obstacles and do something about them. You
      will find that they haven't half the strength you think they have.
      Norman Vincent Peale

470. When you come to a roadblock, take a detour.
      Mary Kay Ash

Decisions

471. In any moment of decision the best thing you can do is the
      right thing, the next best thing is the wrong thing, and the
      worst thing you can do is nothing.
      Theodore Roosevelt

472. It does not take much strength to do things, but it requires
      great strength to decide on what to do.
      Elbert Hubbard

Solutions

473. As long as one keeps searching, the answers come.
      Joan Baez

Hatches, matches and dispatches

Birth

474. At the moment of childbirth, every woman has the same aura of isolation, as though she were abandoned, alone.
Boris Pasternak

475. There is no cure for birth and death save to enjoy the interval.
George Santayana

Engagements

476. An engaged woman is always more agreeable than a disengaged. She is satisfied with herself. Her cares are over, and she feels that she may exert all her powers of pleasing without suspicion. All is safe with a lady engaged; no harm can be done.
Jane Austen

477. Long engagements give people the opportunity of finding out each other's character before marriage, which is never advisable.
Oscar Wilde

Weddings

478. I think weddings is sadder than funerals, because they remind you of your own wedding. You can't be reminded of your own funeral because it hasn't happened. But weddings always make me cry.
Brendan Behan

479. It has been said that a bride's attitude towards her betrothed can be summed up in three words: Aisle. Altar. Hymn.
Frank Muir

Marriage

480. A simple enough pleasure, surely, to have breakfast alone with one's husband, but how seldom married people in the midst of life achieve it.
Anne Morrow Lindbergh

481. A successful marriage requires falling in love many times, always with the same person.
Mignon McLaughlin

482. Before marriage, a man will go home and lie awake all night thinking about something you said; after marriage, he'll go to sleep before you finish saying it.
Helen Rowland

483. I haven't spoken to my wife in years. I didn't want to interrupt her.
Rodney Dangerfield

484. I think like any marriage, especially when you've had divorced parents like myself, you'd want to try even harder to make it work.
Princess Diana

485. I was married by a judge. I should have asked for a jury.
Groucho Marx

486. In olden times sacrifices were made at the altar—a practice which is still continued.
Helen Rowland

487. It is a lovely thing to have a husband and wife developing together and having the feeling of falling in love again. That is what marriage really means: helping one another to reach the full status of being persons, responsible and autonomous beings who do not run away from life.
Paul Tournier

488. I've never been married, but I tell people I'm divorced so they won't think something's wrong with me.
Elayne Boosler

489. Marriage is a framework to preserve friendship. It is valuable because it gives much more room to develop than just living together. It provides a base from which a person can work at understanding himself and another person.
Robertson Davies

490. Marriage is a great institution, but I'm not ready for an institution yet.
Mae West

491. Marriage is a series of desperate arguments people feel passionately about.
Katharine Hepburn

492. My husband and I didn't sign a pre-nuptial agreement. We signed a mutual suicide pact.
Roseanne Barr

493. My wife and I were married in a toilet—it was a marriage of convenience!
Tommy Cooper

494. There were three of us in this marriage, so it was a bit crowded.
Princess Diana
(Interview on Panorama, *1995)*

495. We all have a childhood dream that when there is love, everything goes like silk, but the reality is that marriage requires a lot of compromise.
Raquel Welch

496. We sleep in separate rooms, we have dinner apart, we take separate vacations—we're doing everything we can to keep our marriage together.
Rodney Dangerfield

497. When a girl marries she exchanges the attention of many men for the inattention of one.
Helen Rowland

Bigamy

498. Bigamy is having one husband too many. Monogamy is the same.
Oscar Wilde

499. Bigamy: Only crime where two rites make a wrong.
Bob Hope

500. Q. Do you know the punishment for bigamy? A. Two mothers-in-law.
Anon.

Honeymoons

501. Next to hot chicken soup, a tattoo of an anchor on your chest, and penicillin, I consider a honeymoon one of the most overrated events in the world.
Erma Bombeck

Death and dying

502. Dying is a very dull, dreary affair. And my advice to you is to have nothing whatever to do with it.
William Somerset Maugham

503. It's not that I'm afraid to die, I just don't want to be there when it happens.
Woody Allen

504. Tears are sometimes an inappropriate response to death. When a life has been lived completely honestly, completely successfully, or just completely, the correct response to death's perfect punctuation mark is a smile.
Julie Burchill

505. The bitterest tears shed over graves are for words left unsaid and deeds left undone.
Harriet Beecher Stowe

506. When you have told anyone that you have left him a legacy, the only decent thing is to die at once.
Samuel Butler

Divorce

507. Ah, yes, divorce—from the Latin word meaning to rip out a man's genitals through his wallet.
Robin Williams

508. However often marriage is dissolved, it remains indissoluble. Real divorce, the divorce of heart and nerve and fiber, does not exist, since there is no divorce from memory.
Virgilia Peterson

509. If income tax is the price you have to pay to keep the government on its feet, alimony is the price we have to pay for sweeping a woman off hers.
Groucho Marx

510. Love, the quest; marriage, the conquest; divorce, the inquest.
Helen Rowland

511. The difference between divorce and legal separation is that a legal separation gives a husband time to hide his money.
Johnny Carson

512. When two people decide to get a divorce, it isn't a sign that they "don't understand" one another, but a sign that they have, at last, begun to.
Helen Rowland

Health and healing

Health

513. A healthy body is the guest-chamber of the soul; a sick, its prison.
Francis Bacon

514. I went to my doctor and asked for something for persistent wind. He gave me a kite.
Les Dawson

515. Periods of wholesome laziness, after days of energetic effort, will wonderfully tone up the mind and body.
Grenville Kleiser

516. The higher your energy level, the more efficient your body. The more efficient your body, the better you feel and the more you will use your talent to produce outstanding results.
Anthony Robbins

517. The only reason I would take up jogging is so I could hear heavy breathing again.
Erma Bombeck

518. The only way to keep your health is to eat what you don't want, drink what you don't like, and do what you'd rather not.
Mark Twain

519. You have to stay in shape. My grandmother, she started walking five miles a day when she was 60. She's 97 today and we don't know where the hell she is.
Ellen Degeneras

Healing

520. There are hurts so deep that one cannot reach them or heal them with words.
Kate Seredy

521. When you can't remember why you're hurt, that's when you're healed.
Jane Fonda

Home and housework

522. Cleaning your house while your kids are still growing is like shoveling the walk before it stops snowing.
Phyllis Diller

523. "Home" is any four walls that enclose the right person.
Helen Rowland

524. Housework is a treadmill from futility to oblivion with stop-offs at tedium and counter productivity.
Erma Bombeck

525. I don't know what keeps me down to earth, but it sure isn't ironing. I send mine out.
Cher

526. I hate housework! You make the beds, you do the dishes—and six months later you have to start all over again.
Joan Rivers

527. My theory on housework is, if the item doesn't multiply, smell, catch fire, or block the refrigerator door, let it be. No one else cares. Why should you?
Erma Bombeck

528. No one ever died from sleeping in an unmade bed. I have known mothers who remake the bed after their children do it because there's a wrinkle in the spread or the blanket is on crooked. This is sick.
Erma Bombeck

Humility

529. Humility does not mean thinking less of yourself than of other people, nor does it mean having a low opinion of your own gifts. It means freedom from thinking about yourself at all.
William Temple

530. It's hard to be humble, when you're as great as I am.
Muhammad Ali

Husbands, wives and bachelors

Husbands

531. A husband is what is left of a lover, after the nerve has been extracted.
Helen Rowland

532. A woman must be a genius to create a good husband.
Honoré de Balzac

Wives

533. He that outlives a wife whom he has long loved, sees himself disjoined from the only mind that has the same hopes, and fears, and interest; from the only companion with whom he has shared much good and evil . . .
Samuel Johnson

534. Wives are young men's mistresses, companions for middle age, and old men's nurses.
Francis Bacon

Bachelors

535. A bachelor never quite gets over the idea that he is a thing of beauty and a boy forever.
Helen Rowland

536. A Bachelor of Arts is one who makes love to a lot of women, and yet has the art to remain a bachelor.
Helen Rowland

537. Rich bachelors should be heavily taxed. It is not fair that some men should be happier than others.
Oscar Wilde

Ideas, inspiration and motivation

Ideas

538. A mediocre idea that generates enthusiasm will go further than a great idea that inspires no one.
Mary Kay Ash

539. An idea is a point of departure and no more. As soon as you elaborate it, it becomes transformed by thought.
Pablo Picasso

540. If you do not express your own original ideas, if you do not listen to your own being, you will have betrayed yourself.
Rollo May

541. Keep on the lookout for novel ideas that others have used successfully. Your idea has to be original only in its adaptation to the problem you're working on.
Thomas Edison

542. Man's mind, stretched by a new idea, never goes back to its original dimensions.
Oliver Wendell Holmes

Inspiration

543. Inspirations never go in for long engagements; they demand immediate marriage to action.
Brendan Behan

544. The glow of inspiration warms us; it is a holy rapture.
Ovid

Motivation

545.   Be miserable. Or motivate yourself. Whatever has to be done, it's always your choice.
Wayne Dyer

546.   The whole idea of motivation is a trap. Forget motivation. Just do it. Exercise, lose weight, test your blood sugar, or whatever. Do it without motivation. And then, guess what? After you start doing the thing, that's when the motivation comes and makes it easy for you to keep on doing it.
John C. Maxwell

Individuality and uniqueness

547.   Do not go where the path may lead, go instead where there is no path and leave a trail.
Ralph Waldo Emerson

548.   I decided many years ago to invent myself. I had obviously been invented by someone else—by a whole society—and I didn't like their invention.
Maya Angelou

549.   If you don't design your own life plan, chances are you'll fall into someone else's plan. And guess what they have planned for you? Not much.
Jim Rohn

550.   My great mistake, the fault for which I can't forgive myself, is that one day I ceased my obstinate pursuit of my own individuality.
Oscar Wilde

551.   No matter what age you are, or what your circumstances might be, you are special, and you still have something unique to offer. Your life, because of who you are, has meaning.
Barbara De Angelis

552.   Take your life in your own hands and what happens? A terrible thing: no one to blame.
Erica Jong

553.   The greatest thing in the world is to know how to belong to
       oneself.
       Michel de Montaigne

Intuition, instinct and hunches

Intuition

554.   Intuition comes very close to clairvoyance; it appears to be the
       extrasensory perception of reality.
       Alexis Carrel

555.   Intuition is a suspension of logic due to impatience.
       Rita Mae Brown

Instincts

556.   Trust your instincts. If you have no instincts, trust your
       impulses.
       Noël Coward

Hunches

557.   Trust your hunches. They're usually based on facts filed away
       just below the conscious level.
       Dr. Joyce Brothers

K

Kindness, compassion and warmth

Kindness

558. A warm smile is the universal language of kindness.
William Arthur Ward

559. Constant kindness can accomplish much. As the sun makes ice melt, kindness causes misunderstanding, mistrust, and hostility to evaporate.
Albert Schweitzer

560. Kindness is a language which the deaf can hear, and the blind can read.
Mark Twain

561. Let no one ever come to you without leaving better and happier. Be the living expression of God's kindness: kindness in your face, kindness in your eyes, kindness in your smile.
Mother Teresa

562. When we seek to discover the best in others, we somehow bring out the best in ourselves.
William Arthur Ward

563. When you are kind to someone in trouble, you hope they'll remember and be kind to someone else. And it'll become like a wildfire.
Whoopi Goldberg

Compassion

564. Compassion is not a sloppy, sentimental feeling for people who are underprivileged or sick . . . it is an absolutely practical belief that, regardless of a person's background, ability, or ability to pay, he should be provided with the best that society has to offer.
Neil Kinnock

565. How far you go in life depends on your being tender with the young, compassionate with the aged, sympathetic with the striving and tolerant of the weak and strong. Because someday in your life you will have been all of these.
George Washington Carver

Warmth

566. One looks back with appreciation to the brilliant teachers, but with gratitude to those who touched our human feeling. Curriculum is necessary raw material, but warmth is the vital element for the growing plant and for the soul of the child.
Carl Gustav Jung

Kith and kin

Babies

567. A baby is God's opinion that life should go on.
Carl Sandburg

568. A loud noise at one end and no sense of responsibility at the other.
Ronald Knox

569. Families with babies and families without babies are sorry for each other.
Edgar Watson Howe

570. If you desire to drain to the dregs the fullest cup of scorn and hatred that a fellow human being can pour out for you, let a young mother hear you call dear baby "it."
Jerome K. Jerome

571. The old system of having a baby was much better than the new system, the old system being characterized by the fact that the man didn't have to watch.
Dave Barry

Children and childhood

572. Always be nice to your children because they are the ones who will choose your rest home.
Phyllis Diller

573. Childhood is not only the childhood we really had but also the impressions we formed of it in our adolescence and maturity. That is why childhood seems so long. Probably every period of life is multiplied by our reflections upon the next.
Cesare Pavese

574. Children are curious and are risk takers. They have lots of courage. They venture out into a world that is immense and dangerous. A child initially trusts life and the processes of life.
John Bradshaw

575. Children are supposed to help hold a marriage together. They do this in a number of ways. For instance, they demand so much attention that a husband and wife, concentrating on their children, fail to notice each other's faults.
Richard Armour

576. Children begin by loving their parents. After a time they judge them. Rarely, if ever, do they forgive them.
Oscar Wilde

577. Children have more need of models, than of critics.
Joseph Joubert

578. Discipline is a symbol of caring to a child. He needs guidance. If there is love, there is no such thing as being too tough with a child.
Bette Davis

579. Each day of our lives we make deposits in the memory banks of our children.
Charles Swindoll

580. Few parents nowadays pay any regard to what their children say to them. The old-fashioned respect for the young is fast dying out.
Oscar Wilde

581. Good kids are like sunsets. We take them for granted. Every evening they disappear. Most parents never imagine how hard they try to please us, and how miserable they feel when they think they have failed.
      Erma Bombeck

582. I am convinced that, except in a few extraordinary cases, one form or another of an unhappy childhood is essential to the formation of exceptional gifts.
      Thornton Wilder

583. I have found the best way to give advice to your children is to find out what they want and then advise them to do it.
      Harry S. Truman

584. I see the mind of a 5-year-old as a volcano with two vents: destructiveness and creativeness.
      Sylvia Ashton-Warner

585. If you raise your children to feel that they can accomplish any goal or task they decide upon, you will have succeeded as a parent and you will have given your children the greatest of all blessings.
      Brian Tracy

586. Listen to the desires of your children. Encourage them and then give them the autonomy to make their own decision.
      Denis Waitley

587. One stops being a child when one realizes that telling one's trouble does not make it better.
      Cesare Pavese

588. The best way to make children good is to make them happy.
      Oscar Wilde

589. The childhood shows the man, as morning shows the day.
      John Milton

590. The greatest gift you and your partner can give your children is the example of an intimate, healthy, and loving relationship.
      Barbara De Angelis

591. Train a child in the way he should go, and when he is old he will not turn from it.
[Proverbs 22:6]

592. We are always too busy for our children; we never give them the time or interest they deserve. We lavish gifts upon them; but the most precious gift, our personal association, which means so much to them, we give grudgingly.
Mark Twain

593. We spend the first twelve months of our children's lives teaching them to walk and talk and the next twelve telling them to sit down and shut up.
Phyllis Diller

Adults

594. Adults are obsolete children.
Dr. Seuss

595. What is an adult? A child blown up by age.
Simone de Beauvoir

Mothers

596. A mother is the truest friend we have, when trials, heavy and sudden, fall upon us; when adversity takes the place of prosperity; when friends who rejoice with us in our sunshine, desert us; when troubles thicken around us, still will she cling to us, and endeavor by her kind precepts and counsels to dissipate the clouds of darkness, and cause peace to return to our hearts.
Washington Irving

597. And what the mother sings to the cradle goes all the way to the coffin.
Henry Ward Beecher

598. It is not until you become a mother that your judgment slowly turns to compassion and understanding.
Erma Bombeck

599. Mothers are fonder than fathers of their children because they are more certain they are their own.
      Aristotle

600. When your mother asks, "Do you want a piece of advice?" it's a mere formality. It doesn't matter if you answer yes or no. You're going to get it anyway.
      Erma Bombeck

Fathers

601. A man's desire for a son is usually nothing but the wish to duplicate himself in order that such a remarkable pattern may not be lost to the world.
      Helen Rowland

602. Certain is it that there is no kind of affection so purely angelic as of a father to a daughter. In love to our wives there is desire; to our sons, ambition; but to our daughters there is something which there are no words to express.
      Joseph Addison

603. Fathers and sons arrive at that relationship only by claiming that relationship: that is by paying for it. If the relationship of father to son could really be reduced to biology, the whole earth would blaze with the glory of fathers and sons.
      James Baldwin

Parents

604. If you raise your children to feel that they can accomplish any goal or task they decide upon, you will have succeeded as a parent and you will have given your children the greatest of all blessings.
      Brian Tracy

Family

605. Everybody today seems to be in such a terrible rush, anxious for greater developments and greater riches and so on, so that children have very little time for their parents. Parents have very little time for each other, and in the home begins the disruption of peace of the world.
      Mother Teresa

606. Nobody who has not been in the interior of a family can say
     what the difficulties of any individual of that family may be.
     Jane Austen

Friends and friendship

607. An acquaintance that begins with a compliment is sure to
     develop into a real friendship.
     Oscar Wilde

608. Doing all we can to promote our friend's happiness is better
     than to continually drink to his prosperity.
     Minna Thomas Antrim

609. Friendship is the only cement that will hold the world together.
     Woodrow Wilson

610. It's no good trying to keep up old friendships. It's painful for
     both sides. The fact is, one grows out of people, and the only
     thing is to face it.
     William Somerset Maugham

611. Laughter is not at all a bad beginning for a friendship, and it
     is far the best ending for one.
     Oscar Wilde

612. Sometimes being a friend means mastering the art of timing.
     There is a time for silence. A time to let go and allow people
     to hurl themselves into their own destiny. And a time to
     prepare to pick up the pieces when it's all over.
     Gloria Naylor

613. "Stay" is a charming word in a friend's vocabulary.
     Louisa May Alcott

614. The glory of friendship is not the outstretched hand, nor
     the kindly smile, nor the joy of companionship; it's the
     spiritual inspiration that comes to one when he discovers
     that someone else believes in him and is willing to trust
     him with his friendship.
     Ralph Waldo Emerson

615. The only way to have a friend is to be one.
      Ralph Waldo Emerson

616. True friends stab you in the front.
      Oscar Wilde

617. When a friend is in trouble, don't annoy him by asking if there
      is anything you can do. Think up something appropriate and
      do it.
      Edgar Watson Howe

618. You can make more friends in two months by becoming
      interested in other people than you can in two years by trying
      to get other people interested in you.
      Dale Carnegie

Knowledge and wisdom

Knowledge

619. A little knowledge that acts is worth infinitely more than much
      knowledge that is idle.
      Kahlil Gibran

620. I'd like to be a bigger and more knowledgeable person 10 years
      from now than I am today. I think that, for all of us, as we grow
      older, we must discipline ourselves to continue expanding,
      broadening, learning, keeping our minds active and open.
      Clint Eastwood

621. If a man empties his purse into his head, no one can take it
      from him. An investment in knowledge always pays the best
      interest.
      Benjamin Franklin

622. If you have knowledge, let others light their candles with it.
      Winston Churchill

623. Knowledge is the intellectual manipulation of carefully verified
      observations.
      Sigmund Freud

624. Knowledge rests not upon truth alone, but upon error also.
Carl Gustav Jung

625. There is a great difference between knowing and understanding: you can know a lot about something and not really understand it.
Charles Kettering

Wisdom

626. The doors of wisdom are never shut.
Benjamin Franklin

627. Wisdom is knowing when you can't be wise.
Muhammad Ali

Laughter

628. He who laughs most, learns best.
John Cleese

629. I have seen what a laugh can do. It can transform almost unbearable tears into something bearable, even hopeful.
Bob Hope

630. If you can't make it better, you can laugh at it.
Erma Bombeck

631. Laughter is the tonic, the relief, the surcease for pain.
Charlie Chaplin

632. The person who knows how to laugh at himself will never cease to be amused.
Shirley MacLaine

633. There is a thin line that separates laughter and pain, comedy and tragedy, humor and hurt. And how do you know laughter if there is no pain to compare it with?
Erma Bombeck

634. What may seem depressing or even tragic to one person may seem like an absolute scream to another person, especially if he has had between four and seven beers.
Dave Barry

635. You can turn painful situations around through laughter. If you can find humor in anything—even poverty—you can survive it.
Bill Cosby

636. You grow up the day you have the first real laugh—at yourself.
Ethel Barrymore

Leaders and leadership

637.   A good objective of leadership is to help those who are doing poorly to do well and to help those who are doing well to do even better.
Jim Rohn

638.   A leader is one who knows the way, goes the way and shows the way.
John C. Maxwell

639.   It is very comforting to believe that leaders who do terrible things are, in fact, mad. That way, all we have to do is make sure we don't put psychotics in high places and we've got the problem solved.
Thomas Wolfe

640.   Leaders must be close enough to relate to others, but far enough ahead to motivate them.
John C. Maxwell

Lies and excuses

Lies

641.   Even a liar tells 100 truths to one lie; he has to, to make the lie good for anything.
Henry Ward Beecher

642.   Telling lies is a fault in a boy, an art in a lover, an accomplishment in a bachelor, and second-nature in a married man.
Helen Rowland

Excuses

643.   Nothing is impossible; there are ways that lead to everything, and if we had sufficient will we should always have sufficient means. It is often merely for an excuse that we say things are impossible.
François La Rochefoucauld

644. People are always blaming their circumstances for what they are. I don't believe in circumstances. The people who get on in this world are the people who get up and look for the circumstances they want, and, if they can't find them, make them.
George Bernard Shaw

Life and living

645. "Life"
Life is an opportunity, benefit from it.
Life is beauty, admire it.
Life is bliss, taste it.
Life is a dream, realise it.
Life is a challenge, meet it.
Life is a duty, complete it.
Life is a game, play it.
Life is costly, care for it.
Life is wealth, keep it.
Life is love, enjoy it.
Life is mystery, know it.
Life is a promise, fulfil it.
Life is sorrow, overcome it.
Life is a song, sing it.
Life is a struggle, accept it.
Life is tragedy, confront it.
Life is an adventure, dare it.
Life is luck, make it.
Life is too precious, do not destroy it.
Life is life, fight for it.
Mother Teresa

646. Don't sweat the petty things, and don't pet the sweaty things.
George Carlin

647. Don't go around saying the world owes you a living. The world owes you nothing. It was here first.
Mark Twain

648. Life can be wildly tragic at times, and I've had my share. But whatever happens to you, you have to keep a slightly comic attitude. In the final analysis, you have got not to forget to laugh.
Katharine Hepburn

649. Life is a gift, and it offers us the privilege, opportunity, and responsibility to give something back by becoming more.
Anthony Robbins

650. Life is a great big canvas; throw all the paint on it you can.
Danny Kaye

651. Life is a lively process of becoming.
Douglas MacArthur

652. Life isn't one straight line. Most of us have to be transplanted, like a tree, before we blossom.
Louise Nevelson

653. Live in such a way that you would not be ashamed to sell your parrot to the town gossip.
Will Rogers

654. Living your life the way you want to live it is the most important thing, so if you have to pay small prices along the way it's not important.
Cher

655. The drama of life begins with a wail and ends with a sigh.
Minna Thomas Antrim

656. The good life, as I conceive it, is a happy life. I do not mean that if you are good you will be happy; I mean that if you are happy you will be good.
Bertrand Russell

657. The more you praise and celebrate your life, the more there is in life to celebrate.
Oprah Winfrey

658. The place to improve the world is first in one's own heart and head and hands.
Robert M. Pirsig

659. The value of life lies, not in the length of days, but in the use we make of them; a man may live long, yet live very little. Satisfaction in life depends not on the number of your years, but on your will.
Michel de Montaigne

660. To live is the rarest thing in the world. Most people exist, that is all.
Oscar Wilde

661. To live is to function. That is all there is in living.
Oliver Wendell Holmes

Love, kissing and affection

Love

662. All love shifts and changes. I don't know if you can be wholeheartedly in love all the time.
Julie Andrews

663. If you want a love message to be heard, it has got to be sent out. To keep a lamp burning, we have to keep putting oil in it.
Mother Teresa

664. In love the paradox occurs that two beings become one and yet remain two.
Erich Fromm

665. Love ceases to be a pleasure, when it ceases to be a secret.
Aphra Behn

666. Love is an act of endless forgiveness, a tender look which becomes a habit.
Peter Ustinov

667. Love is composed of a single soul inhabiting two bodies.
Aristotle

668. Love is like the measles; we all have to go through with it.
Jerome K. Jerome

669. Love takes off masks that we fear we cannot live without and know we cannot live within.
James Baldwin

670. Those who are faithful know only the trivial side of love: it is the faithless who know love's tragedies.
Oscar Wilde

671. When love turns away, now, I don't follow it. I sit and suffer, unprotesting, until I feel the tread of another step.
Sylvia Ashton-Warner

Kissing

672. A kiss is a lovely trick designed by nature to stop speech when words become superfluous.
Ingrid Bergman

673. To a woman the first kiss is just the end of the beginning, but to a man it is the beginning of the end.
Helen Rowland

Affection

674. Every gift, though it be small, is in reality great if given with affection.
Pindar

Luck and opportunity

Luck

675. Luck is a dividend of sweat. The more you sweat, the luckier you get.
Ray Kroc

676. Luck is a matter of preparation meeting opportunity.
Oprah Winfrey

677. What we call luck is the inner man externalized. We make things happen to us.
Robertson Davies

Opportunity

678. Chance is always powerful.
      Let your hook be always cast.
      In the pool where you least expect it,
      will be a fish.
      Ovid

679. If a window of opportunity appears, don't pull down the
      shade.
      Tom Peters

680. Opportunities are like sunrises. If you wait too long, you miss
      them.
      William Arthur Ward

M

Memories and memory

681. But each day brings its petty dust our soon-choked souls to fill,
     and we forget because we must, and not because we will.
     Matthew Arnold

682. I can understand that memory must be selective, else it would
     choke on the glut of experience. What I cannot understand is
     why it selects what it does.
     Virgilia Peterson

683. Memory is the scribe of the soul.
     Aristotle

684. No memory is ever alone; it's at the end of a trail of memories,
     a dozen trails that each have their own associations.
     Louis L'Amour

685. Memory . . . is the diary that we all carry about with us.
     Oscar Wilde

686. We do not remember days, we remember moments. The
     richness of life lies in memories we have forgotten.
     Cesare Pavese

687. Why is it that our memory is good enough to retain the least
     triviality that happens to us, and yet not good enough to
     recollect how often we have told it to the same person?
     François La Rochefoucauld

Men

688. Men are what their mothers made them.
     Ralph Waldo Emerson

689. Young men want to be faithful and are not; old men want to
      be faithless and cannot.
      Oscar Wilde

Men and women

690. A successful man is one who makes more money than his wife
      can spend. A successful woman is one who can find such a man.
      Lana Turner

691. If you want anything said, ask a man. If you want something
      done, ask a woman.
      Margaret Thatcher

692. Man has his will, but woman has her way.
      Oliver Wendell Holmes

693. Men and women belong to different species, and
      communication between them is a science still in its infancy.
      Bill Cosby

694. Men are allowed to have passion and commitment for their
      work . . . a woman is allowed that feeling for a man, but not
      her work.
      Barbra Streisand

695. Sometimes I wonder if men and women really suit each other.
      Perhaps they should live next door and just visit now and then.
      Katharine Hepburn

696. To control a man a woman must first control herself.
      Minna Thomas Antrim

697. What Women Want: To be loved, to be listened to, to be
      desired, to be respected, to be needed, to be trusted, and
      sometimes, just to be held. What Men Want: Tickets for the
      world series.
      Dave Barry

698. When men and women agree, it is only in their conclusions;
      their reasons are always different.
      George Santayana

699. When men and women are able to respect and accept their differences then love has a chance to blossom.
John Gray

Mental health issues, psychiatrists and psychiatry, and psychoanalysis

Anxiety

700. "Anxiety" describes a particular state of expecting the danger or preparing for it, even though it may be an unknown one. "Fear" requires a definite object of which to be afraid. "Fright", however, is the name we give to the state a person gets into when he has run into danger without being prepared for it; it emphasizes the factor of surprise.
Sigmund Freud

701. Anxiety is a thin stream of fear trickling through the mind. If encouraged, it cuts a channel into which all other thoughts are drained.
Robert Albert Bloch

Breakdown

702. Madness need not be all breakdown. It may also be break-through. It is potential liberation and renewal as well as enslavement and existential death.
R. D. Laing

703. The world breaks everyone, and afterward many are strong at the broken places.
Ernest Hemingway

Depression

704. Depression is rage spread thin.
George Santayana

705. Geez, if I could get through to you, kiddo, that depression is
      not sobbing and crying and giving vent, it is plain and simple
      reduction of feeling. Reduction, see? Of all feeling. People who
      keep stiff upper lips find that it's damn hard to smile.
      Judith Guest

706. If we admit our depression openly and freely, those around us
      get from it an experience of freedom rather than the
      depression itself.
      Rollo May

707. It's a recession when your neighbor loses his job; it's a
      depression when you lose yours.
      Harry S. Truman

708. Sometimes one has simply to endure a period of depression for
      what it may hold of illumination if one can live through it,
      attentive to what it exposes or demands.
      May Sarton

709. When mothers talk about the depression of the empty nest,
      they're not mourning the passing of all those wet towels on
      the floor, or the music that numbs your teeth, or even the
      bottle of capless shampoo dribbling down the shower drain.
      They're upset because they've gone from supervisor of a child's
      life to a spectator. It's like being the vice president of the
      United States.
      Erma Bombeck

710. When women are depressed, they either eat or go shopping.
      Men invade another country. It's a whole different way of
      thinking.
      Elayne Boosler

Neurosis and psychosis

711. Doubt is to certainty as neurosis is to psychosis. The neurotic is
      in doubt and has fears about persons and things; the psychotic
      has convictions and makes claims about them. In short, the
      neurotic has problems, the psychotic has solutions.
      Thomas Szasz

712.   For the rational, psychologically healthy man, the desire for
       pleasure is the desire to celebrate his control over reality. For
       the neurotic, the desire for pleasure is the desire to escape
       from reality.
       Nathaniel Branden

713.   Neurosis is always a substitute for legitimate suffering.
       Carl Gustav Jung

714.   Neurosis is no worse than a bad cold; you ache all over, and
       it's made you a mess, but you won't die from it.
       Mignon McLaughlin

715.   Neurosis is the inability to tolerate ambiguity.
       Sigmund Freud

716.   Work and love, these are the basics. Without them there is
       neurosis.
       Theodor Reik

Sanity and insanity

717.   Insanity is often the logic of an accurate mind overtaxed.
       Oliver Wendell Holmes

718.   The experience and behaviour that gets labelled schizophrenic
       is a special strategy that a person invents in order to live in an
       unlivable situation.
       R. D. Laing

719.   The statistics on sanity are that one out of every four
       Americans is suffering from some form of mental illness. Think
       of your three best friends. If they're okay, then it's you.
       Rita Mae Brown

720.   Why is it when we talk to God, we're said to be praying—but
       when God talks to us, we're schizophrenic?
       Lily Tomlin

Psychiatrists and psychiatry

721.   A psychiatrist asks a lot of expensive questions your wife asks
       for nothing.
       Joey Adams

722. Hello, welcome to the psychiatric hotline.
     If you are obsessive-compulsive, press 1 repeatedly.
     If you are co-dependent, please ask someone to press 2.
     If you have multiple personalities, press 3, 4, 5, and 6.
     If you are paranoid-delusional, we know who you are and what you want. Just stay on the line so we can trace the call.
     If you are schizophrenic, listen carefully and a little voice will tell you which button to press.
     If you are manic-depressive, it doesn't matter which number you press. No one will answer.
     Anon.

723. I always say shopping is cheaper than a psychiatrist.
     Tammy Faye Bakker

724. I told my psychiatrist that everyone hates me. He said I was being ridiculous—everyone hasn't met me yet.
     Rodney Dangerfield

Psychoanalysis

725. A wonderful discovery, psychoanalysis. Makes quite simple people feel they're complex.
     S.N. Behrman

726. The aim of psychoanalysis is to relieve people of their neurotic unhappiness so that they can be normally unhappy.
     Sigmund Freud

Morality

727. Moral excellence comes about as a result of habit. We become just by doing just acts, temperate by doing temperate acts, brave by doing brave acts.
     Aristotle

728. Morality is simply the attitude we adopt towards people we personally dislike.
     Oscar Wilde

729.   When the sun comes up, I have morals again.
       Elayne Boosler

730.   Your morals are like roads through the Alps. They make these
       hairpin turns all the time.
       Erica Jong

Music

731.   Music is the language of the spirit. It opens the secret of life
       bringing peace, abolishing strife.
       Kahlil Gibran

O

Optimism and Pessimism

Optimism

732. I am an optimist, but I'm an optimist who carries a raincoat.
Harold Wilson

733. I have become my own version of an optimist. If I can't make it through one door, I'll go through another door—or I'll make a door. Something terrific will come no matter how dark the present.
Joan Rivers

734. In these times you have to be an optimist to open your eyes when you wake in the morning.
Carl Sandburg

735. One of the things I learned the hard way was that it doesn't pay to get discouraged. Keeping busy and making optimism a way of life can restore your faith in yourself.
Lucille Ball

736. Optimism is the faith that leads to achievement. Nothing can be done without hope and confidence.
Helen Keller

737. Optimism. The doctrine or belief that everything is beautiful, including what is ugly.
Ambrose Bierce

Pessimism

738. A pessimist is one who, when he has a choice of two evils, chooses both.
Oscar Wilde

739. Dwelling on the negative simply contributes to its power.
Shirley MacLaine

740. I don't believe in pessimism. If something doesn't come up the way you want, forge ahead. If you think it's going to rain, it will.
Clint Eastwood

741. Most of the shadows of this life are caused by standing in one's own sunshine.
Ralph Waldo Emerson

742. No pessimist ever discovered the secrets of the stars, or sailed to an uncharted land, or opened a new heaven to the human spirit.
Helen Keller

Optimism and Pessimism

743. The optimist proclaims that we live in the best of all possible worlds; and the pessimist fears this is true.
James Branch Cabell

744. The optimist sees the rose and not its thorns; the pessimist stares at the thorns, oblivious to the rose.
Kahlil Gibran

745. The pessimist complains about the wind; the optimist expects it to change; the realist adjusts the sails.
William Arthur Ward

746. The pessimist sees difficulty in every opportunity. The optimist sees the opportunity in every difficulty.
Winston Churchill

747. Two men look out through the same bars:
One sees the mud, and one the stars.
Frederick Langbridge

P

Pain and suffering

748. Affliction comes to us all not to make us sad, but sober; not
to make us sorry, but wise; not to make us despondent, but
by its darkness to refresh us, as the night refreshes the day;
not to impoverish, but to enrich us, as the plough enriches
the field.
Henry Ward Beecher

749. I do not believe that sheer suffering teaches. If suffering alone
taught, all the world would be wise; since everyone suffers. To
suffering must be added mourning, understanding, patience,
love, openness and the willingness to remain vulnerable.
Anne Morrow Lindbergh

750. If you are distressed by anything external, the pain is not due
to the thing itself, but to your estimate of it; and this you have
the power to revoke at any moment.
Marcus Aurelius Antoninus

751. It's odd that you can get so anesthetized by your own pain or
your own problem that you don't quite fully share the hell of
someone close to you.
Lady Bird Johnson

752. The only antidote to mental suffering is physical pain.
Karl Marx

753. There is a great deal of pain in life and perhaps the only pain
that can be avoided is the pain that comes from trying to
avoid pain.
R. D. Laing

754. We are healed of a suffering only by experiencing it in full.
Marcel Proust

755. When we honestly ask ourselves which person in our lives means the most to us, we often find that it is those who, instead of giving advice, solutions, or cures, have chosen rather to share our pain and touch our wounds with a warm and tender hand.
Henri Nouwen

756. Your pain is the breaking of the shell that encloses your understanding.
Kahlil Gibran

Past, present and future

757. Few of us ever live in the present, we are forever anticipating what is to come or remembering what has gone.
Louis L'Amour

758. I can feel guilty about the past, apprehensive about the future, but only in the present can I act. The ability to be in the present moment is a major component of mental wellness.
Abraham Maslow

759. If we open a quarrel between the past and the present, we shall find we have lost the future.
Winston Churchill

760. Life is divided into three terms—that which was, which is, and which will be. Let us learn from the past to profit by the present and from the present to live better for the future.
William Wordsworth

761. The best way to predict the future is to create it.
Peter Drucker

762. The most effective way to ensure the value of the future is to confront the present courageously and constructively.
Rollo May

763. Those who cannot remember the past are condemned to repeat it.
George Santayana

764. Who controls the past controls the future. Who controls the present controls the past.
George Orwell

765. Yesterday is gone. Tomorrow has not yet come. We have only today. Let us begin.
Mother Teresa

Patience

766. I'm extraordinarily patient provided I get my own way in the end.
Margaret Thatcher

767. Never cut a tree down in the wintertime. Never make a negative decision in the low time. Never make your most important decisions when you are in your worst moods. Wait. Be patient. The storm will pass. The spring will come.
Robert Schuller

768. No greater thing is created suddenly, any more than a bunch of grapes or a fig. If you tell me that you desire a fig, I answer you that there must be time. Let it first blossom, then bear fruit, then ripen.
Epictetus

769. Our patience will achieve more than our force.
Edmund Burke

People

770. All the people like us are we,
And everyone else is They.
Rudyard Kipling

771. Most people are other people. Their thoughts are someone else's opinions, their lives a mimicry, their passions a quotation.
Oscar Wilde

772.   People are very open-minded about new things—as long as
       they're exactly like the old ones.
       Charles Kettering

773.   There are three types of people in this world: those who make
       things happen, those who watch things happen and those who
       wonder what happened. We all have a choice. You can decide
       which type of person you want to be. I have always chosen to
       be in the first group.
       Mary Kay Ash

Perfectionism

774.   Certain flaws are necessary for the whole. It would seem
       strange if old friends lacked certain quirks.
       Johann Wolfgang von Goethe

775.   Every human being must thus be viewed according to what it
       is good for; for none of us, no, not one, is perfect; and were we
       to love none who had imperfections, this world would be a
       desert for our love.
       Thomas Jefferson

776.   Have no fear of perfection—you'll never reach it.
       Salvador Dali

777.   Perfectionism is a dangerous state of mind in an imperfect world.
       Robert Hillyer

778.   Ring the bells that still can ring, forget your perfect offering.
       There is a crack in everything, that's how the light gets in.
       Leonard Cohen

Poverty and money

Poverty

779.   Anyone who has ever struggled with poverty knows how
       extremely expensive it is to be poor.
       James Baldwin

780. Having been poor is no shame, but being ashamed of it, is.
Benjamin Franklin

781. If you teach a poor young man to shave himself, and keep his razor in order, you may contribute more to the happiness of his life than in giving him a thousand guineas.
Benjamin Franklin

Money

782. Creditors have better memories than debtors.
Benjamin Franklin

783. Draw your salary before spending it.
Artemus Ward

784. He who multiplies riches, multiplies cares.
Benjamin Franklin

785. If you pay peanuts, you get monkeys.
James Goldsmith (Attrib.)

786. Money cannot buy health, but I'd settle for a diamond-studded wheelchair.
Dorothy Parker

787. Money can't buy friends, but you can get a better class of enemy.
Spike Milligan

788. Money is like love; it kills slowly and painfully the one who withholds it, and enlivens the other who turns it on his fellow man.
Kahlil Gibran

789. Money is like muck, not good except it be spread.
Francis Bacon

790. Money is the root of all evil, and yet it is such a useful root that we cannot get on without it any more than we can without potatoes.
Louisa May Alcott

791. Money never made a man happy yet, nor will it. The more a man has, the more he wants. Instead of filling a vacuum, it makes one.
Benjamin Franklin

792. Money, it turned out, was exactly like sex: you thought of nothing else if you didn't have it and thought of other things if you did.
James Baldwin

793. No one can earn a million dollars honestly.
William Jennings Bryan

794. Pennies do not come from heaven—they have to be earned here on earth.
Margaret Thatcher

795. Saving is a fine thing. Especially when your parents have done it for you.
Winston Churchill

796. There is only one thing for a man to do who is married to a woman who enjoys spending money, and that is enjoy earning it.
Ogden Nash

Power, powerlessness and empowerment

Power

797. Power tends to corrupt, and absolute power corrupts absolutely.
Lord Acton

798. Where love rules, there is no will to power; and where power predominates, there love is lacking. The one is the shadow of the other.
Carl Gustav Jung

Powerlessness

799. A voice is a human gift; it should be cherished and used, to utter fully human speech as possible. Powerlessness and silence go together.
Margaret Atwood

Empowerment

800. Alone we can do so little; together we can do so much.
Helen Keller

801. I think education is power. I think that being able to communicate with people is power. One of my main goals on the planet is to encourage people to empower themselves.
Oprah Winfrey

802. Women have to harness their power – it's absolutely true. It's just learning not to take the first no. And if you can't go straight ahead, you go around the corner.
Cher

Principles

803. It is always easier to fight for one's principles than to live up to them.
Alfred Adler

804. It is personalities not principles that move the age.
Oscar Wilde

Problems

805. A problem well stated is a problem half solved.
Charles Kettering

806. If we can really understand the problem, the answer will come out of it, because the answer is not separate from the problem.
Jiddu Krishnamurti

807. It is only because of problems that we grow mentally and spiritually.
M. Scott Peck

808. People become attached to their burdens sometimes more than the burdens are attached to them.
George Bernard Shaw

809. Problems are not the problem; coping is the problem. Coping is the outcome of self-worth, rules of the family systems, and links to the outside world.
Virginia Satir

810. Problems are to the mind what exercise is to the muscles, they toughen and make strong.
Norman Vincent Peale

811. The only people without problems are in cemeteries.
Anthony Robbins

812. To solve any problem, here are three questions to ask yourself: First, what could I do? Second, what could I read? And third, who could I ask?
Jim Rohn

813. Walk away from it until you're stronger. All your problems will be there when you get back, but you'll be better able to cope.
Lady Bird Johnson

814. We are all faced with a series of great opportunities brilliantly disguised as unsolvable problems.
John W. Gardner

Procrastination

815. Even if you are on the right track, you'll get run over if you just sit there.
Will Rogers

816. Never put off till tomorrow what may be done day after tomorrow just as well.
Mark Twain

817. Procrastination is one of the most common and deadliest of diseases and its toll on success and happiness is heavy.
Wayne Dyer

818.   Procrastination is the fear of success. People procrastinate because they are afraid of the success that they know will result if they move ahead now. Because success is heavy, carries a responsibility with it, it is much easier to procrastinate and live on the "someday I'll" philosophy.
Denis Waitley

819.   Procrastination is the thief of time.
Edward Young

820.   While we are postponing, life speeds by.
Seneca

Q

Quality and quantity

821. It is quality rather than quantity that counts.
     Seneca

822. The quality of an individual is reflected in the standards they set for themselves.
     Ray Kroc

Questions and answers

823. A prudent question is one-half of wisdom.
     Francis Bacon

824. Hypothetical questions get hypothetical answers.
     Joan Baez

825. I keep six honest serving-men
     (They taught me all I knew);
     Their names are What and Why and When
     And How and Where and Who.
     Rudyard Kipling [following the story "Elephant's Child" in "Just So Stories"]

826. Quality questions create a quality life. Successful people ask better questions, and as a result, they get better answers.
     Anthony Robbins

827. Questions provide the key to unlocking our unlimited potential.
     Anthony Robbins

Quotations

828. I love quotations because it is a joy to find thoughts one might have, beautifully expressed with much authority by someone recognized wiser than oneself.
Marlene Dietrich

829. I quote others in order to better express myself.
Michel de Montaigne

830. It is a good thing for an uneducated man to read books of quotations.
Winston Churchill

831. The wisdom of the wise, and the experience of ages, may be preserved by quotation.
Benjamin Disraeli

832. When a thing has been said and well, have no scruple. Take it and copy it.
Anatole France

R

Reality

833. A theory must be tempered with reality.
Jawaharlal Nehru

834. I believe that unarmed truth and unconditional love will have the final word in reality. That is why right, temporarily defeated, is stronger than evil triumphant.
Martin Luther King, Jr.

835. I made some studies, and reality is the leading cause of stress amongst those in touch with it. I can take it in small doses, but as a lifestyle, I found it too confining.
Jane Wagner

836. Reality is the crutch for people who can't cope with drugs.
Lily Tomlin

837. Set up as an ideal the facing of reality as honestly and as cheerfully as possible.
Karl A. Menninger

838. Sometimes legends make reality, and become more useful than the facts.
Salman Rushdie

839. Television is actually closer to reality than anything in books. The madness of TV is the madness of human life.
Camille Paglia

840. The atmosphere of libraries, lecture rooms and laboratories is dangerous to those who shut themselves up in them too long. It separates us from reality like a fog.
Alexis Carrel

841. The people who say you are not facing reality actually mean that you are not facing their idea of reality. Reality is above all else a variable. With a firm enough commitment, you can sometimes create a reality which did not exist before.
Margaret Halsey

842. There's no reality except the one contained within us. That's why so many people live an unreal life. They take images outside them for reality and never allow the world within them to assert itself.
Hermann Hesse

843. We cast away priceless time in dreams, born of imagination, fed upon illusion, and put to death by reality.
Judy Garland

844. We live in a fantasy world, a world of illusion. The great task in life is to find reality.
Iris Murdoch

845. We take our shape, it is true, within and against that cage of reality bequeathed us at our birth; and yet it is precisely through our dependence on this reality that we are most endlessly betrayed.
James Baldwin

846. Whatever you believe with feeling becomes your reality.
Brian Tracy

Refusing and requesting

847. A "No" uttered from deepest conviction is better and greater than a "Yes" merely uttered to please, or what is worse, to avoid trouble.
Mahatma Gandhi

848. Asking is the beginning of receiving. Make sure you don't go to the ocean with a teaspoon. At least take a bucket so the kids won't laugh at you.
Jim Rohn

849. If you don't ask, you don't get.
     Mahatma Gandhi

850. One-half the troubles of this life can be traced to saying yes too quickly and not saying no soon enough.
     Josh Billings

851. You don't always get what you ask for, but you never get what you don't ask for . . . unless it's contagious!
     Beverly Sills

Relationships

852. Don't smother each other. No one can grow in the shade.
     Leo Buscaglia

853. The easiest kind of relationship for me is with ten thousand people. The hardest is with one.
     Joan Baez

854. The only real security in a relationship lies neither in looking back in nostalgia, nor forward in dread or anticipation, but living in the present relationship and accepting it as it is now.
     Anne Morrow Lindbergh

855. The quality of your life is the quality of your relationships.
     Anthony Robbins

Risks

856. Risk! Risk anything! Care no more for the opinion of others, for those voices. Do the hardest thing on earth for you. Act for yourself. Face the truth.
     Katherine Mansfield

857. The person who risks nothing, does nothing, has nothing, is nothing, and becomes nothing. He may avoid suffering and sorrow, but he simply cannot learn and feel and change and grow and love and live.
     Leo Buscaglia

Self related

Self-actualization

858.   What a man can be, he must be. This need we call self-actualization.
Abraham Maslow

Self-awareness

859.   A human being is only interesting if he's in contact with himself. I learned you have to trust yourself, be what you are, and do what you ought to do the way you should do it. You have got to discover you, what you do, and trust it.
Barbra Streisand

860.   A moment's insight is sometimes worth a life's experience.
Oliver Wendell Holmes

861.   I want, by understanding myself, to understand others. I want to be all that I am capable of becoming.
Katherine Mansfield

862.   Nothing said to us, nothing we can learn from others, reaches us so deep as that which we find in ourselves.
Theodor Reik

863.   One of the greatest moments in anybody's developing experience is when he no longer tries to hide from himself but determines to get acquainted with himself as he really is.
Norman Vincent Peale

864.   What is necessary to change a person is to change his awareness of himself.
Abraham Maslow

Self-concept and self-worth

865. An individual's self-concept is the core of his personality. It affects every aspect of human behavior: the ability to learn, the capacity to grow and change. A strong, positive self-image is the best possible preparation for success in life.
Dr. Joyce Brothers

866. Feelings of worth can flourish only in an atmosphere where individual differences are appreciated, mistakes are tolerated, communication is open, and rules are flexible—the kind of atmosphere that is found in a nurturing family.
Virginia Satir

867. It is of practical value to learn to like yourself. Since you must spend so much time with yourself you might as well get some satisfaction out of the relationship.
Norman Vincent Peale

868. Until you value yourself, you won't value your time. Until you value your time, you will not do anything with it.
M. Scott Peck

Self-confidence

869. Self-confidence is the first requisite to great undertakings.
Samuel Johnson

870. The way to develop self-confidence is to do the thing you fear and get a record of successful experiences behind you. Destiny is not a matter of chance, it is a matter of choice; it is not a thing to be waited for, it is a thing to be achieved.
William Jennings Bryan

Self-development

871. If you wish to achieve worthwhile things in your personal and career life, you must become a worthwhile person in your own self-development.
Brian Tracy

872. Invest three percent of your income in yourself (self-development) in order to guarantee your future.
Brian Tracy

873. No one can develop freely in this world and find a full life without feeling understood by at least one person.
Paul Tournier

874. The real voyage of discovery consists not in seeking new landscapes, but in having new eyes.
Marcel Proust

Self-esteem

875. If rejection destroys your self-esteem, you're letting others hold you as an emotional hostage.
Brian Tracy

876. Self-esteem is the quality of the relationship we have with ourselves.
Jan Sutton

Self-growth

877. Self-reverence, self-knowledge, self-control. These three alone lead life to sovereign power.
Alfred Lord Tennyson

878. We need 4 hugs a day for survival. We need 8 hugs a day for maintenance. We need 12 hugs a day for growth.
Virginia Satir

Self-respect

879. He that respects himself is safe from others. He wears a coat of mail that none can pierce.
Henry Wadsworth Longfellow

880. Would that there were an award for people who come to understand the concept of enough. Good enough. Successful enough. Thin enough. Rich enough. Socially responsible enough. When you have self-respect you have enough . . .
Gail Sheehy

Selfishness

881.   It is easier to do one's duty to others than to one's self. If you do your duty to others, you are considered reliable. If you do your duty to yourself, you are considered selfish.
Thomas Szasz

882.   Selfishness is not living as one wishes to live; it is asking others to live as one wishes to live. And unselfishness is letting other people's lives alone, not interfering with them. Selfishness always aims at uniformity of type.
Oscar Wilde

Sense of humour and wit

Sense of humour

883.   A person without a sense of humor is like a wagon without springs—jolted by every pebble in the road.
Henry Ward Beecher

884.   A well-developed sense of humor is the pole that adds balance to your steps as you walk the tightrope of life.
William Arthur Ward

Wit

885.   Everything is funny, as long as it's happening to somebody else.
Will Rogers

886.   The next best thing to being witty one's self, is to be able to quote another's wit.
Christian Nestell Bovee

887.   Wit ought to be a glorious treat, like caviar. Never spread it about like marmalade.
Noël Coward

Senses

888. Nothing can cure the soul but the senses, just as nothing can cure the senses but the soul.
      Oscar Wilde

889. Nothing recalls the past so potently as a smell.
      Winston Churchill

890. Of all the senses, sight must be the most delightful.
      Helen Keller

891. Our senses don't deceive us: our judgement does.
      Johann Wolfgang von Goethe

892. Our sight is the most perfect and most delightful of all our senses. It fills the mind with the largest variety of ideas, converses with its objects at the greatest distance, and continues the longest in action without being tired or satiated . . .
      Joseph Addison

893. Smell is a potent wizard that transports us across thousands of miles and all the years we have lived.
      Helen Keller

Sex and sexual innuendo

894. All this fuss about sleeping together. For physical pleasure I'd sooner go to my dentist any day.
      Evelyn Waugh

895. Clinton lied. A man might forget where he parks or where he lives, but he never forgets oral sex, no matter how bad it is.
      Barbara Bush

896. Hey, don't knock masturbation! It's sex with someone I love.
      Woody Allen

897. I remember the first time I had sex—I kept the receipt.
      Groucho Marx

898. I'll come and make love to you at five o'clock. If I'm late start without me.
      Tallulah Bankhead

899. I'm at the age where food has taken the place of sex in my life. In fact, I've just had a mirror put over my kitchen table.
Rodney Dangerfield

900. Is that a gun in your pocket, or are you just glad to see me?
Mae West

901. I've tried several varieties of sex. The conventional position makes me claustrophobic and the others give me a stiff neck or lockjaw.
Tallulah Bankhead

902. Macho does not prove mucho.
Zsa Zsa Gabor

903. Masturbation: the primary sexual activity of mankind. In the nineteenth century it was a disease; in the twentieth, it's a cure.
Thomas Szasz

904. My brain: it's my second favorite organ.
Woody Allen

905. My wife is a sex object—every time I ask for sex, she objects.
Les Dawson

906. Pornography is the attempt to insult sex, to do dirt on it.
D. H. Lawrence

907. Remember, if you smoke after sex you're doing it too fast.
Woody Allen

908. Seems to me the basic conflict between men and women, sexually, is that men are like firemen. To men, sex is an emergency, and no matter what we're doing we can be ready in two minutes. Women, on the other hand, are like fire. They're very exciting, but the conditions have to be exactly right for it to occur.
Jerry Seinfeld

909. The human race has been set up. Someone, somewhere, is playing a practical joke on us. Apparently, women need to feel loved to have sex. Men need to have sex to feel loved. How do we ever get started?
Billy Connolly

910. The only time my wife and I had a simultaneous orgasm was when the judge signed the divorce papers.
Woody Allen

911. There is hardly anyone whose sexual life, if it were broadcast, would not fill the world at large with surprise and horror.
William Somerset Maugham

912. There's a new medical crisis. Doctors are reporting that many men are having allergic reactions to latex condoms. They say they cause severe swelling. So what's the problem?
Dustin Hoffman

913. There's only one good test of pornography. Get twelve normal men to read the book, and then ask them, "Did you get an erection?" If the answer is "Yes" from a majority of the twelve, then the book is pornographic.
W. H. Auden

914. When modern woman discovered the orgasm it was (combined with modern birth control) perhaps the biggest single nail in the coffin of male dominance.
Eva Figes

915. Women might be able to fake orgasms. But men can fake whole relationships.
Sharon Stone

Silence and solitude

Silence

916. In the silence of night I have often wished for just a few words of love from one man, rather than the applause of thousands of people.
Judy Garland

917. Silence is a great help to the seeker after truth. In the attitude of silence, the soul finds the path in a clearer light, and what is elusive and deceptive resolves itself into crystal clearness. Our life is a long and arduous quest after truth, and the soul requires inward restfulness to attain its full height.
Mahatma Gandhi

Solitude

918. I live in that solitude which is painful in youth, but delicious in the years of maturity.
Albert Einstein

919. Solitude: A good place to visit, but a poor place to stay.
Josh Billings

Sleep

920. A man can do only what a man can do. But if he does that each day he can sleep at night and do it again the next day.
Albert Schweitzer

921. If you can't sleep, then get up and do something instead of lying there and worrying. It's the worry that gets you, not the loss of sleep.
Dale Carnegie

Smiling

922. A smile is the light in your window that tells others that there is a caring, sharing person inside.
Denis Waitley

923. Smiling is infectious,
You catch it like the flu,
When someone smiled at me today,
I started smiling too.

I passed around the corner
And someone saw my grin . . .
When he smiled I realized
I'd passed it on to him.

I thought about that smile,
Then I realized its worth.
A single smile, just like mine
Could travel round the earth.

So, if you feel a smile begin,
Don't leave it undetected . . .
Let's start an epidemic quick,
And get the world infected!
Anon.

Special occasions

Christmas

924. Bloody Christmas, here again.
Let us raise a loving cup:
Peace on earth, goodwill to men,
And make them do the washing up.
Wendy Cope

925. There's nothing sadder in this world than to awake Christmas morning and not be a child.
Erma Bombeck

Mother's Day

926. Spend at least one Mother's Day with your respective (mother-in-law) before you decide on marriage. If a man gives his mother a gift certificate for a flu shot, dump him.
Erma Bombeck

Vacations

927. On vacations: We hit the sunny beaches where we occupy ourselves keeping the sun off our skin, the saltwater off our bodies and the sand out of our belongings.
Erma Bombeck

Success and failure

Success

928. If you wish success in life, make perseverance your bosom friend, experience your wise counselor, caution your elder brother and hope your guardian genius.
Joseph Addison

929. Success is a great deodorant. It takes away all your past smells.
Elizabeth Taylor

930. Success is doing what you want to do, when you want, where you want, with whom you want, as much as you want.
Anthony Robbins

931. The secret of success is learning how to use pain and pleasure instead of having pain and pleasure use you. If you do that, you're in control of your life. If you don't, life controls you.
Anthony Robbins

932. There are no shortcuts to any place worth going.
Beverly Sills

933. What is success? I think it is a mixture of having a flair for the thing that you are doing; knowing that is it not enough, that you have got to have hard work and a certain sense of purpose.
Margaret Thatcher

934. You have reached the pinnacle of success as soon as you become uninterested in money, compliments, or publicity.
Thomas Wolfe

Success and failure

935. I don't know the key to success, but the key to failure is trying to please everybody.
Bill Cosby

936. People fail forward to success.
Mary Kay Ash

937. Success and failure are both difficult to endure. Along with success come drugs, divorce, fornication, bullying, travel, meditation, medication, depression, neurosis and suicide. With failure comes failure.
Joseph Heller

Failure

938. Failure is not fatal. Only failure to get back up is.
John C. Maxwell

939. Failure should be our teacher, not our undertaker. Failure is delay, not defeat. It is a temporary detour, not a dead end. Failure is something we can avoid only by saying nothing, doing nothing, and being nothing.
Denis Waitley

940. I don't fear failure. I only fear the slowing up of the engine inside of me which is pounding, saying, "Keep going, someone must be on top, why not you?"
George S. Patton

941. I have not failed. I've just found 10,000 ways that won't work.
Thomas Edison

942. You may be disappointed if you fail, but you are doomed if you don't try.
Beverly Sills

Suicide

943. He who does not accept and respect those who want to reject life does not truly accept and respect life itself.
Thomas Szasz

944. Let them think what they liked, but I didn't mean to drown myself. I meant to swim till I sank, but that's not the same thing.
Joseph Conrad

945. To run away from trouble is a form of cowardice and, while it is true that the suicide braves death, he does it not for some noble object but to escape some ill.
Aristotle

T

Temptation

946. All men are tempted. There is no man that lives that cannot be broken down, provided it is the right temptation, put in the right spot.
Henry Ward Beecher

947. Lead me not into temptation; I can find the way myself.
Rita Mae Brown

The mind and brain

948. A contented mind is the greatest blessing a man can enjoy in this world.
Joseph Addison

949. A person will be just about as happy as they make up their minds to be.
Abraham Lincoln

950. Few minds wear out; more rust out.
Christian Nestell Bovee

951. I not only use all the brains that I have, but all that I can borrow.
Woodrow Wilson

952. It is not enough to have a good mind. The main thing is to use it well.
René Descartes

953. It is the sign of a dull mind to dwell upon the cares of the body, to prolong exercise, eating and drinking, and other bodily functions. These things are best done by the way; all your attention must be given to the mind.
Epictetus

954. Mind unemployed is mind un-enjoyed.
     Christian Nestell Bovee

955. Most of the time we think we're sick, it's all in the mind.
     Thomas Wolfe

956. Our limitations and success will be based, most often, on your
     own expectations for ourselves. What the mind dwells upon,
     the body acts upon.
     Denis Waitley

957. The absence of alternatives clears the mind marvelously.
     Henry Kissinger

958. The mind is the limit. As long as the mind can envision the
     fact that you can do something, you can do it, as long as you
     really believe 100 percent.
     Arnold Schwarzenegger

959. The truth is that we can learn to condition our minds, bodies,
     and emotions to link pain or pleasure to whatever we choose.
     By changing what we link pain and pleasure to, we will
     instantly change our behaviors.
     Anthony Robbins

960. The voice of the intellect is a soft one, but it does not rest till it
     has gained a hearing.
     Sigmund Freud

961. To get the most out of your life, plant in your mind seeds of
     constructive power that will yield fruitful results.
     Grenville Kleiser

The unknown

962. We tend not to choose the unknown, which might be a shock
  . or a disappointment or simply a little difficult to cope with.
     And yet it is the unknown with all its disappointments and
     surprises that is the most enriching.
     Anne Morrow Lindbergh

Time management

963. Do not squander time for that is the stuff life is made of.
Benjamin Franklin

964. God gave you a gift of 86,400 seconds today. Have you used one to say "thank you"?
William Arthur Ward

965. Once you have mastered time, you will understand how true it is that most people overestimate what they can accomplish in a year—and underestimate what they can achieve in a decade!
Anthony Robbins

966. Time is an equal opportunity employer. Each human being has exactly the same number of hours and minutes every day. Rich people can't buy more hours. Scientists can't invent new minutes. And you can't save time to spend it on another day. Even so, time is amazingly fair and forgiving. No matter how much time you've wasted in the past, you still have an entire tomorrow.
Denis Waitley

967. Time is the coin you have in life. It is the only coin you have, and only you can determine how it will be spent. Be careful lest you let other people spend it for you.
Carl Sandburg

V

Violence

968. A riot is the language of the unheard.
Martin Luther King, Jr.

969. Deeds of violence in our society are performed largely by those trying to establish their self-esteem, to defend their self-image, and to demonstrate that they, too, are significant.
Rollo May

970. The ultimate weakness of violence is that it is a descending spiral, begetting the very thing it seeks to destroy. Instead of diminishing evil, it multiplies it.
Martin Luther King, Jr.

971. Violence arises not out of superfluity of power but out of powerlessness.
Rollo May

Virus

972. Virus is a Latin word used by doctors to mean "your guess is as good as mine".
Bob Hope

Visitors

973. My evening visitors, if they cannot see the clock, should find the time in my face.
Ralph Waldo Emerson

974. When one pays a visit it is for the purpose of wasting other people's time, not one's own.
Oscar Wilde

Widows

975. A widow is a fascinating being with the flavor of maturity, the spice of experience, the piquancy of novelty, the tang of practiced coquetry, and the halo of one man's approval.
Helen Rowland

Winners and losers

976. Every time you win, it diminishes the fear a little bit. You never really cancel the fear of losing; you keep challenging it.
Arthur Ashe

977. Losers spend time explaining why they lost. Losers spend their lives thinking about what they're going to do. They rarely enjoy doing what they're doing.
Eric Berne

978. The winners in life think constantly in terms of I can, I will, and I am. Losers, on the other hand, concentrate their waking thoughts on what they should have or would have done, or what they can't do.
Denis Waitley

Women

979. A woman is like a tea bag—you can't tell how strong she is until you put her in hot water.
Nancy Reagan

980. At work, you think of the children you've left at home. At home, you think of the work you've left unfinished. Such a struggle is unleashed within yourself, your heart is rent.
Golda Meir

981. God gave women intuition and femininity. Used properly, the combination easily jumbles the brain of any man I've ever met.
Farrah Fawcett

982. I am a woman in process. I'm just trying like everybody else. I try to take every conflict, every experience, and learn from it. Life is never dull.
Oprah Winfrey

983. I believe that what women resent is not so much giving herself in pieces as giving herself purposelessly.
Anne Morrow Lindbergh

984. I like to help women help themselves, as that is, in my opinion, the best way to settle the woman question. Whatever we can do and do well we have a right to, and I don't think anyone will deny us.
Louisa May Alcott

985. Most women set out to change a man, and when they have changed him they do not like him.
Marlene Dietrich

986. On the day when it will be possible for woman to love not in her weakness but in strength, not to escape herself but to find herself, not to abase herself but to assert herself—on that day love will become for her, as for man, a source of life . . .
Simone de Beauvoir

987. The freedom that women were supposed to have found in the Sixties largely boiled down to easy contraception and abortion; things to make life easier for men, in fact.
Julie Burchill

988. The great question which I have not been able to answer, despite my 30 years of research into the feminine soul, is "What does a woman want?"
Sigmund Freud

989. These impossible women! How they do get around us! The poet was right: Can't live with them, or without them.
      Aristophanes

990. To be successful, a woman has to be much better at her job than a man.
      Golda Meir

991. We women are callow fledglings as compared with the wise old birds who manipulate the political machinery, and we still hesitate to believe that a woman can fill certain positions in public life as competently and adequately as a man.
      Eleanor Roosevelt

992. Women are at last becoming persons first and wives second, and that is as it should be.
      May Sarton

993. Women like silent men. They think they're listening.
      Marcel Achard

Work and workforce

Work

994. Einstein's Three Rules of Work: 1) Out of clutter find simplicity; 2) From discord find harmony; 3) In the middle of difficulty lies opportunity.
      Albert Einstein

995. I like work: it fascinates me. I can sit and look at it for hours. I love to keep it by me: the idea of getting rid of it nearly breaks my heart.
      Jerome K. Jerome

996. Pleasure in the job puts perfection in the work.
      Aristotle

997. The price one pays for pursuing any profession or calling is an intimate knowledge of its ugly side.
      James Baldwin

Workforce

998.   If you want creative workers, give them enough time to play.
John Cleese

999.   The world is moved along not only by the mighty shoves of its heroes, but also by the aggregate of the tiny pushes of each honest worker.
Helen Keller

1000.   We treat our people like royalty. If you honor and serve the people who work for you, they will honor and serve you.
Mary Kay Ash

Internet references

Please note: At the time this page was prepared all sites, databases, and search engines listed, were active.

Amusing Quotes
http://www.amusingquotes.com/

Bartleby Library – "Great Books Online"
Includes:
Bartlett's Familiar Quotations
Simpson's Contemporary Quotations
The Columbia World of Quotations
http://www.bartleby.com/

Ask Jeeves
http://www.ask.com/

BrainyQuote
http://www.brainyquote.com/

Comedy Zone
http://www.comedy-zone.net/guide/quotes.htm

Creative Quotations
http://creativequotations.com

Dead or Alive?
Tracks whether famous people are alive or deceased
http://www.deadoraliveinfo.com/dead.nsf/pages/main

Famous Quotations Network
http://www.famous-quotations.com/

Famous quotes
http://home.att.net/~quotations

GaleNet Biography Resource Center
Password required.
http://infotrac.galegroup.com/default.

GIGA quotes
http://www.giga-usa.com/

Google
http://www.google.com/

Here's looking at you! The know yourself seminar
http://www.leaderworks.com/knowyourself/quotes.html

Humorous Quotes – Jest for Pun
http://www.workinghumor.com/quotes/

Joke Monster quotes
http://www.jokemonster.com/quotes/

Lines to Live By...
http://www.trends.net/~roversct/Quotes/

Motivating Moments
http://www.motivateus.com/

MotivationalQuotes.Com
http://www.motivationalquotes.com/

Quotable Quotes
http://www.quotablequotes.net/

Quotable Women – An Archive of Memorable Quotes by Women
http://www.wendy.com/women/quotations.html

Quotation Central
http://www.quotationscentral.com/

QuotationReference.com
http://www.quotationreference.com/

Quote Me On It
http://www.quotemeonit.com/

Quote World
http://www.quoteworld.org/

QuoteGallery.com
http://www.quotegallery.com/

Quoteland.com
http://quoteland.com/

QuoteNotes®
http://brightpath.hypermart.net/QN/QNIndex.htm

Quotez
http://www.quotations.co.uk/

The Quotation Archive
http://www.aphids.com/quotes/index.shtml

The Quotations Home Page
http://www.theotherpages.org/quote.html

The Quotations Page
http://www.quotationspage.com/

The Quote Cache
http://quotes.prolix.nu/

The Quote Garden
http://www.quotegarden.com/

Think Exist
www.thinkexist.com

ToInspire.com
http://www.toinspire.com/

TPCN – Quotation Center (Cyber Nation)
http://www.cyber-nation.com/victory/quotations/

WorldofQuotes.com
http://www.worldofquotes.com/

Books by authors listed in 1000 Pocket Positives

Details of books published by authors listed in this book are available online at Amazon (see below), and other major online bookstores.

Amazon.co.uk: http://www.amazon.co.uk

Amazon.com: http://www.amazon.com

Further reading

Cassell Dictionary of Humorous Quotes, Nigel Rees (Cassell reference, 1998).

Great Quotes from Great Leaders, Peggy Anderson (ed), (Career Press, 1997).

The Book of Positive Quotations, John Cook (compiler), (Fairview Press, 1997).

The Oxford Dictionary of Humorous Quotations, Ned Sherrin (ed), (Oxford University Press, 2002).

The Oxford Dictionary of Quotations, Elizabeth Knowles (ed), (Oxford University Press, 1999).

The Penguin Dictionary of Modern Humorous Quotations, Fred Metcalf (ed), (Penguin Books, 2003).

The Wicked Wit of Winston Churchill, Dominique Enright (compiler), (Andrews McMeel Publishing, 2001).

The Wit and Wisdom of Oscar Wilde: A Treasury of Quotations, Anecdotes, and Observations, Oscar Wilde (Crown Publications, 1999).

The Women's Book of Positive Quotations, Leslie Ann Gibson (compiler), (Fairview Press, 2002).

Author index

Ashe, Arthur
US tennis player, AIDS spokesperson,
    writer (1943–1993)
    Giving 56 : 450
    Winners and losers 124 : 976

Ashton-Warner, Sylvia
New Zealand educator, novelist, poet
    (1908–1984)
    Children and childhood 73 : 584
    Love 84 : 671

Astor, Nancy
American-born English stateswoman
    (1879–1964)
    Age and ageing 11 : 92

Atkinson, Ron
English soccer pundit. Ex-player.
Manchester United manager. (1939)
    Football 55 : 447

Atwood, Margaret
Canadian novelist, poet (1939)
    Powerlessness 100 : 799

Auden, W. H.
English-born US poet, dramatist,
    editor (1907–1973)
    Sex and sexual innuendo
        115 : 913

Austen, Jane
English author (1775–1817)
    Engagements 59 : 476
    Family 76 : 606

Bacon, Francis
British philosopher (1561–1626)
    Abilities 1 : 4
    Advice 10 : 84
    Revenge 55 : 443
    Health 63 : 513
    Wives 66 : 534

Money 99 : 789
Questions and answers
    104 : 823

Baez, Joan
US folksinger, political activist (1941)
    Equality 42 : 329
    Solutions 58 : 473
    Questions and answer 104 : 824
    Relationships 108 : 853

Bailey, Philip James
English poet (1816–1902)
    Deeds 7 : 53

Bakker, Tammy Faye
US TV evangelist (1942)
    Psychiatrists and psychiatry
        91 : 723

Baldwin, James
US novelist, essayist (1924–1987)
    Hate 53 : 426
    Fathers 75 : 603
    Love 83 : 669
    Poverty 98 : 779
    Money 100 : 792
    Reality 107 : 845
    Work 126 : 997

Ball, Lucille
US comedy actress (1911–1989)
    Optimism 93 : 735

Balzac, Honoré de
French author (1799–1850)
    Equality 41 : 327
    Husbands 65 : 532

Bankhead, Tallulah
US actress (1903–1968)
    Diaries 21 : 174
    Sex and sexual innuendo
        113 : 898

Conrad, Joseph
Polish novelist, short-story writer
 (1857–1924)
  Suicide 119 : 944

Cooper, Tommy
Welsh-English comedian, magician
 (1922–1984)
  Marriage 61 : 493

Cope, Wendy
English writer (1945)
  Christmas 117 : 924

Cosby, Bill
US comedian, actor, philosopher,
 author (1937)
  Laughter 79 : 635
  Men and women 87 : 693
  Success and failure 118 : 935

Covey, Stephen R.
US consultant, author (1932–)
  Listening 28 : 229

Coward, Noël
English playwright, actor, composer
 (1899–1973)
  Alcohol 8 : 62
  Criticism 35 : 287
  Instincts 69 : 556
  Wit 112 : 887

Crawford, Cindy
US model (1966)
  *Appearance, breasts, fashion and
   style* 13 : 106

Dali, Salvador
Spanish painter, printmaker
 (1904–1989)
  Perfectionism 98 : 776

Dangerfield, Rodney
US comedian, actor (1921)
  Weight 38 : 306
  Marriage 60 : 483; 61 : 496
  Psychiatrists and psychiatry
   91 : 724
  Sex and sexual innuendo
   114 : 899

Darwin, Charles
English naturalist, author
 (1809–1882)
  Habit 9 : 72
  Thinking and thought 19 : 158

Davies, Robertson
Canadian author (1913–1995)
  Writers and writing 15 : 129
  Eyes 43 : 339
  Marriage 61 : 489
  Luck 84 : 677

Davis, Bette
US actress (1908–1989)
  Children and childhood 72 : 578

Dawson, Les
English comedian (1934–1993)
  Health 63 : 514
  Sex and sexual innuendo
   114 : 905

De Angelis, Barbara
US psychotherapist, author (1951)
  Anger 48 : 379
  Individuality and uniqueness
   68 : 551
  Children and childhood 73 : 590

De Vries, Peter
US novelist, editor (1910–1993)
  Gluttony 33 : 304

Degeneras, Ellen
US comedian, actress, author (1958)
Health 64 : 519

Descartes, René
French philosopher, mathematician,
scientist (1596–1650)
The mind and brain 120 : 952

Diana, Princess of Wales
English princess, (1961–1997)
Feelings and emotions – general
45 : 354
Marriage 60 : 484; 61 : 494

Dietrich, Marlene
German-born US actress, singer
(1901–1992)
Quotations 105 : 828
Women 125 : 985

Diller, Phyllis
US comedienne (1917)
Home and housework 64 : 522
Children and childhood 72 : 572;
74 : 593

Disney, Walt
US movie producer, illustrator
(1901–1966)
Curiosity 35 : 282

Disraeli, Benjamin
British prime minister (1804–1881)
Order 23 : 190
Anticipation 48 : 386
Quotations 105 : 831

Dix, Dorothy
US journalist, writer (1870–1951)
Communication: verbal and non-verbal 26 : 212

Douglas, Helen Gahagan
US actress, opera singer, politician
(1900–1980)
Feelings and emotions – general
46 : 357

Drucker, Peter
Austrian-born US writer, educator,
management consultant (1909)
Communication: verbal and non-verbal 27 : 216
Past, present and future 96 : 761

Dryden, John
English poet, dramatist, critic
(1631–1700)
Beauty 20 : 171

Dyer, Wayne
US psychologist, author (1940)
Appreciation and approval
14 : 116
Loneliness 54 : 440
Motivation 68 : 545
Procrastination 102 : 817

Eastwood, Clint
US actor, director (1930)
Prejudice 37 : 298
Knowledge 77 : 620
Pessimism 94 : 740

Edison, Thomas
US inventor (1847–1931)
Genius 2 : 10
Ideas 67 : 541
Failure 119 : 941

Einstein, Albert
German-born US physicist (1879–1955)
Eyes 42 : 335

Franklin, Benjamin
US statesman, author, inventor,
   scientist (1706–1790)
   Talent 2 : 14
   Habit 9 : 71
   Enthusiasm 25 : 206
   Anger 48 : 381
   Anticipation 48 : 384
   Pride 54 : 442
   Knowledge 77 : 621
   Wisdom 78 : 626
   Poverty 99 : 780, 781
   Money 99 : 782, 784, 791
   Time management 122 : 963

Freud, Clement
English raconteur, wit, author (1924)
   Abstinence 3 : 21

Freud, Sigmund
Austrian psychoanalyst (1856–1939)
   Thinking and thought 19 : 161
   Mistakes 44 : 343
   Knowledge 77 : 623
   Anxiety 88 : 700
   Neurosis and psychosis 90 : 715
   Psychoanalysis 91 : 726
   The mind and brain 121 : 960
   Women 125 : 988

Friday, Nancy
US author (1938)
   Anger 47 : 367

Fromm, Erich
German-born US psychoanalyst
   (1900–1980)
   Grief and loss 51 : 412
   Love 83 : 664

Gabor, Zsa Zsa
Hungarian-born US actress (1917)
   Sex and sexual innuendo 114 : 902

Gandhi, Indira
Indian political leader (1917–1984)
   Anger 48 : 383

Gandhi, Mahatma
Indian philosopher, activist, religious
   leader (1869–1948)
   Abilities 1 : 5
   Disagreements 15 : 122
   Change 23 : 184
   Criticism 36 : 292
   Teaching 41 : 323
   Anger 46 : 364
   Refusing and requesting
      107 : 847; 108 : 849
   Silence 115 : 917

Gardner, John W.
US writer, government official
   (1912–2002)
   Creativity 34 : 278
   Fear 50 : 403
   Problems 102 : 814

Garland, Judy
US actress, singer (1922–1969)
   Loneliness 54 : 435
   Reality 107 : 843
   Silence 115 : 916

Gay, John
English poet, dramatist, author
   (1685–1732)
   Envy 49 : 391

Gibran, Kahlil
Lebanese-born US poet, artist,
   writer, philosopher (1883–1931)
   Learning 40 : 318
   Giving 56 : 453
   Knowledge 77 : 619
   Music 92 : 731
   Optimism and pessimism 94 : 744

Hoffman, Dustin
US actor (1937)
Sex and sexual innuendo 115 : 912

Holmes, Oliver Wendell
US writer, physician (1809–1894)
Listening 27 : 223
Prejudice 37 : 301
Ideas 67 : 542
Life and living 83 : 661
Men and women 87 : 692
Sanity and insanity 90 : 717
Self-awareness 109 : 860

Hooper, Ellen Sturgis
US poet (1816–1841)
Beauty 20 : 167

Hope, Bob
US comedian, actor (1903–2003)
Age and ageing 11 : 93; 12 : 98
Helping others 56 : 456
Bigamy 62 : 499
Laughter 79 : 629
Virus 123 : 972

Howe, Edgar Watson
US editor, novelist, essayist
(1853–1937)
Babies 71 : 569
Friends and friendship 77 : 617

Hubbard, Elbert
US writer, editor (1856–1915)
Abilities 1 : 3
Criticism 36 : 291
Decisions 58 : 472

Huerta, Dolores
US-Chicana? activist, labor leader
(1930)
Forgiveness 51 : 408

Hume, David
Scottish philosopher, historian
(1711–1776)
Beauty 20 : 165

Huxley, Aldous
English novelist, critic (1894–1963)
Genius 2 : 12

Irving, Washington
US short-story writer, essayist
(1783–1859)
Alcohol 8 : 65
Change 22 : 180
*Communication: verbal and
non-verbal* 27 : 217
Anger 46 : 363
Mothers 74 : 596

Jackson, Andrew
7th US President (1767–1845)
Action 6 : 44

James, William
US psychologist, philosophical writer
(1842–1910)
Acceptance 4 : 24
Attitude 16 : 136; 17 : 141

Jefferson, Thomas
3rd US president, educator (1743–1826)
Words 29 : 240
Perfectionism 98 : 775

Jerome, Jerome K.
English author (1859–1927)
Truth 31 : 256
Feelings and emotions – general
45 : 352
Babies 71 : 570
Love 83 : 668
Work 126 : 995

Johnson, Lady Bird
US first lady (1912)
    Pain and suffering 95 : 751
    Problems 102 : 813

Johnson, Samuel
British lexicographer, author
    (1709–1784)
    Absence 3 : 18
    Perseverance 33 : 271
    Criticism 35 : 284
    Grief and loss 51 : 414
    Wives 66 : 533
    Self-confidence 110 : 869

Jong, Erica
US poet, novelist, essayist (1942)
    Talent 2 : 13
    Advice 10 : 81
    Judgement 36 : 294
    Fear 50 : 397
    Jealousy 53 : 432
    Individuality and uniqueness
        68 : 552
    Morality 92 : 730

Joubert, Joseph
French essayist, moralist
    (1754–1824)
    Children and childhood 72 : 577

Jung, Carl Gustav
Swiss psychologist, psychiatrist
    (1875–1961)
    Acceptance 4 : 29
    Addiction 7 : 56
    Personality 25 : 204
    Conflict 32 : 260
    Confrontation 32 : 261
    Feelings and emotions – general
        46 : 360
    Hate 52 : 423

    Warmth 71 : 566
    Knowledge 78 : 624
    Neurosis and psychosis 90 : 713
    Power 100 : 798

Karr, Alphonse
French journalist, novelist
    (1808–1890)
    Character 24 : 200

Kaye, Danny
US actor, comedian (1913–1987)
    Life and living 82 : 650

Keller, Helen
US blind and deaf author, lecturer,
    (1880–1968)
    Accomplishments 4 : 30
    Beauty 20 : 168
    Character 24 : 196
    Dignity 38 : 308
    Happiness 52 : 420
    Optimism 93 : 736
    Pessimism 94 : 742
    Empowerment 101 : 800
    Senses 113 : 890, 893
    Workforce 127 : 999

Kennedy, John F.
35th US president (1917–1963)
    Action 6 : 47

Kennedy, Joseph P.
US financier, diplomat,
    (1888–1969)
    Action 6 : 50
    Jealousy 54 : 433

Kennedy, Robert F.
US politician, lawyer (1925–1968)
    Achievements 5 : 37
    Dreams 39 : 311

Kent, Dorothea
US actress (1916–1990)
Age and ageing 11 : 88

Kerr, Jean
US humorist, author, playwright
(1923–2003)
Creating a crisis 34 : 276
Diet 38 : 303

Kettering, Charles
US engineer, inventor (1876–1958)
Knowledge 78 : 625
People 98 : 772
Problems 101 : 805

King, Billie Jean
US tennis player, women's rights
advocate (1943)
Attitude 17 : 142

King, Martin Luther, Jr.
US clergyman, civil rights leader
(1929–1968)
Age and ageing 12 : 96
Conscience 32 : 262
Prejudice 36 : 297
Anger 47 : 377
Hate 53 : 425
Reality 106 : 834
Violence 123 : 968, 970

Kingsley, Charles
English clergyman, writer (1819–1875)
Enthusiasm 26 : 209

Kinnock, Neil
Welsh politician (1942)
Compassion 70 : 564

Kipling, Rudyard
British author (1865–1936)

Words 29 : 242
People 97 : 770
Questions and answers 104 : 825

Kissinger, Henry
US government official (1923)
The mind and brain 121 : 957

Kleiser, Grenville
US author (1868–1953)
Character 24 : 194
Health 63 : 515
The mind and brain 121 : 961

Knox, Ronald
British Catholic priest, writer
(1888–1957)
Babies 71 : 568

Krishnamurti, Jiddu
Indian philosopher, author
(1895–1986)
Listening 28 : 227
Fear 50 : 404
Problems 101 : 806

Kroc, Ray
US businessman, founder of
McDonald's corporation
(1902–1984)
Education 40 : 317
Luck 84 : 675
Quality and quantity 104 : 822

Kübler-Ross, Elisabeth
Swiss-US psychiatrist (1926)
Mistakes 45 : 349

Kundera, Milan
Czech-born French novelist,
playwright, poet (1929)
Shame and humiliation 55 : 445

La Rochefoucauld, François
French classical author (1613–1680)
Abilities 1 : 6
Listening 28 : 228
Excuses 80 : 643
Memories and memory 86 : 687

Laing, R.D.
English psychiatrist (1927–1989)
Breakdown 88 : 702
Sanity and insanity 90 : 718
Pain and suffering 95 : 753

Lamartine, Alphonse De
French poet, historian, diplomat
(1790–1869)
Grief and loss 51 : 409

L'Amour, Louis
US author (1908–1988)
Talking 29 : 234
Memories and memory 86 : 684
Past, present and future 96 : 757

Landers, Ann
US author, advice columnist
(1918–2002)
Alcohol 8 : 64

Langbridge, Frederick
English poet, religious writer
(1849–1923)
Optimism and pessimism 94 : 747

Lawrence, D.H.
English novelist, short-story writer,
poet (1885–1930)
Acceptance 4 : 27
Sex and sexual innuendo
114 : 906

Lec, Stanislaw J.
Polish aphorist, poet, satirist

(1909–1966)
Guilt 52 : 415

Lee, Gypsy Rose
US burlesque actress (1914–1970)
*Appearance, breasts, fashion
and style* 13 : 105

Lincoln, Abraham
16th US president, lawyer
(1809–1865)
Age and ageing 11 : 89
Character 24 : 198
The mind and brain 120 : 949

Lindbergh, Anne Morrow
US writer (1906–2001)
*Communication: verbal and non-
verbal* 26 : 211
Truth 31 : 258
Happiness 52 : 418
Loneliness 54 : 438
Giving 56 : 452
Marriage 60 : 480
Pain and suffering 95 : 749
Relationships 108 : 854
The unknown 121 : 962
Women 125 : 983

Longfellow, Henry Wadsworth
US poet, educator (1807–1882)
Words 29 : 237
Self-respect 111 : 879

MacArthur, Douglas
US Army general (1880–1964)
Age and ageing 12 : 97
Life and living 82 : 651

MacLaine, Shirley
US actress, dancer, writer (1934)
Laughter 79 : 632
Pessimism 94 : 739

Mencken, H. L.
US editor, literary critic (1880–1956)
   Criticism 35 : 283

Menninger, Karl A.
US psychiatrist, author (1893–1990)
   Attitudes 16 : 134
   Listening 28 : 226
   Reality 106 : 837

Milligan, Spike
English actor, comedian (1918–2002)
   Money 99 : 787

Milton, John
English poet, essayist (1608–1674)
   Children and childhood 73 : 589

Montaigne, Michel de
French author (1533–1592)
   Arguments 14 : 119
   Individuality and uniqueness
     69 : 553
   Life and living 82 : 659
   Quotations 105 : 829

Mother Teresa
Serbian-born Indian nun, missionary
   (1910–1997)
   Words 29 : 238
   Judgement 36 : 295
   Loneliness 54 : 436
   Kindness 70 : 561
   Family 75 : 605
   Life and living 81 : 645
   Love 83 : 663
   Past, present and future 97 : 765

Muir, Frank
English comedian, author
   (1920–1998)
   Weddings 59 : 479

Murdoch, Iris
Irish author (1919–1999)
   Reality 107 : 844

Nash, Ogden
US poet (1902–1971)
   Money 100 : 796

Naylor, Gloria
US writer, educator (1950)
   Friends and friendship 76 : 612

Neal, Patricia
US stage and screen actress (1926)
   Attitude 16 : 131
   Teaching 40 : 320

Nehru, Jawaharlal
Indian political leader (1889–1964)
   Reality 106 : 833

Nelson, Paula
US economist (1945)
   Equality 42 : 331

Nevelson, Louise
Russian-born US sculptor, painter
   (1899–1988)
   Life and living 82 : 652

Newton, Sir Isaac
English mathematician, philosopher,
   scientist (1642–1727)
   Achievements 5 : 35

Niebuhr, Reinhold
US theologian, author (1892–1971)
   Acceptance 4 : 26

Nightingale, Earl
US motivational author (1921–1989)
   Attitude 17 : 139

Peters, Tom
US consultant, author (1942)
  Opportunity 85 : 679

Peterson, Virgilia
US writer, literary critic (1904–1966)
  Divorce 63 : 508
  Memories and memory 86 : 682

Picasso, Pablo
Spanish painter, sculptor
  (1881–1973)
  Action 6 : 42
  Diaries 21 : 175
  Ideas 67 : 539

Pindar
Greek poet (c. 518B.C.–438 B.C.)
  Affection 84 : 674

Pirsig, Robert M.
US novelist, writer (1928)
  Goals 58 : 467
  Life and living 82 : 658

Pliny the Elder
Roman naturalist, encyclopedist
  (c. 23 A.D. –c. 79 A.D.)
  Envy 49 : 390

Plutarch
Greek philosopher, biographer
  (A.D. c. 46–c. 120?)
  Listening 27 : 224

Powell, Colin
US general (1937)
  Anger 47 : 370

Proust, Marcel
French author (1871–1922)
  Pain and suffering 95 : 754
  Self-development 111 : 874

Proverbs
  Action 6 : 43
  Education 40 : 316
  Children and childhood 74 : 591

Rabelais, François
French writer, doctor, humanist
  (c. 1494– c. 1553)
  Truth 31 : 257

Raleigh, Sir Walter
English navigator, historian, courtier
  (c. 1552–1618)
  Talking 29 : 236

Reagan, Nancy
US first lady, actress (1921)
  Women 124 : 979

Reik, Theodor
Vienna-born US psychoanalyst,
  author (1888–1969)
  Genius 2 : 11
  Neurosis and psychosis 90 : 716
  Self-awareness 109 : 862

Rich, Adrienne
US poet, educator (1929)
  Pride 54 : 441

Richter, Jean Paul
German novelist (1763–1825)
  Absence 3 : 17

Rivers, Joan
US comedian, talk show host,
  writer (1937)
  Anger 46 : 366
  Home and housework 65 : 526
  Optimism 93 : 733

Robbins, Anthony

US writer, motivational speaker
(1960)
   Change 22 : 179; 23 : 186
   Commitment 25 : 205
   Communication: verbal and non-verbal 27 : 218
   Determination 33 : 267
   Destiny 39 : 313
   Goals 57 : 463
   Health 64 : 516
   Life and living 82 : 649
   Problems 102 : 811
   Questions and answers
      104 : 826, 827
   Relationships 108 : 855
   Success 118 : 930, 931
   The mind and brain 121 : 959
   Time management 122 : 965

Rogers, Will

US actor, humorist (1879–1935)
   Praise 30 : 250
   Life and living 82 : 653
   Procrastination 102 : 815
   Wit 112 : 885

Rohn, Jim

US success author (1930)
   Change 23 : 185
   Communication: verbal and non-verbal 26 : 213
   Words 29 : 243
   Envy 49 : 392
   Happiness 52 : 419
   Sadness 55 : 444
   Individuality and uniqueness
      68 : 549
   Leaders and leadership 80 : 637
   Problems 102 : 812
   Refusing and requesting
      107 : 848

Roosevelt, Eleanor

US first lady, author, social reformer
(1884–1962)
   Character 24 : 195
   Curiosity 35 : 280, 281
   Criticism 35 : 286
   Inferiority 53 : 430
   Women 126 : 991

Roosevelt, Franklin D.

32nd US president (1882–1945)
   Doubts 7 : 55
   Adversity and prosperity 10 : 78

Roosevelt, Theodore

26th US president (1858–1919)
   Action 6 : 41
   Ambition 12 : 101
   Decisions 58 : 471

Rowland, Helen

English-US writer (1876–1950)
   Marriage 60 : 482, 486; 61 : 497
   Divorce 63 : 510, 512
   Home and housework 64 : 523
   Husbands 65 : 531
   Bachelors 66 : 535, 536
   Fathers 75 : 601
   Lies 80 : 642
   Kissing 84 : 673
   Widows 124 : 975

Rumsfeld, Donald

US politician, 21st Secretary of
Defense (1932)
   Criticism 35 : 288
   Mistakes 44 : 346

Rushdie, Salman

India-born English novelist (1947)
   Reality 106 : 838

Seredy, Kate
Hungarian-born American
   children's writer, illustrator
   (1899–1975)
   Healing 64 : 520

Seuss, Dr.
US writer, illustrator (1904–1991)
   Adults 74 : 594

Seymour, Jane
English actress (1951)
   Beauty 20 : 164

Shadwell, Thomas
English dramatist, poet (1642–1692)
   Words 30 : 244

Shakespeare, William
English dramatist, poet
   (1564–1616)
   Alcohol 8 : 63

Shankly, Bill
Scottish football manager
   (1913–1981)
   Football 55 : 449

Shaw, George Bernard
Irish-born English author (1856–1950)
   Alcohol 7 : 58
   Arguments 14 : 120
   Excuses 81 : 644
   Problems 101 : 808

Sheehy, Gail
US writer, journalist, editor (1937)
   Change 22 : 176
   Self-respect 111 : 880

Sills, Beverly
US opera singer (1929)
   Anger 46 : 365

Refusing and requesting 108 : 851
Success 118 : 932
Failure 119 : 942

Sinatra, Frank
US singer, actor (1915–1998)
   Abstinence 3 : 20
   Feelings and emotions – general
      45 : 353

Sinetar, Marsha
US author, educator (19??)
   Change 22 : 177

Smith, Hannah Whitall
US evangelist, reformer, suffragist,
   author (1832–1911)
   Advice 11 : 87

Socrates
Greek philosopher
   (469?B.C.–399?B.C.)
   Teaching 41 : 322

Sophocles
Greek poet, dramatist
   (496B.C.–406B.C.)
   Fear 50 : 401
   Grief and loss 51 : 411

Spurgeon, Charles
English preacher (1834–1892)
   Perseverance 33 : 270

Stanhope, Philip Dormer
English statesman, author
   (1694–1773)
   Advice 10 : 80

Steiger, Rod
US actor (1925–2002)
   Shame and humiliation 55 : 446

Stevenson, Robert Louis
Scottish author, poet (1850–1894)
Action 6 : 46

Stone, Sharon
US actress (1958)
Appearance, breasts, fashion and style 13 : 104
Sex and sexual innuendo 115 : 915

Stone, W. Clement
US businessman, philanthropist (1902– 2002)
Attitude 17 : 143

Stowe, Harriet Beecher
US author (1811–1896)
Adversity and prosperity 10 : 79
Death and dying 62 : 505

Streisand, Barbra
US actress, singer (1942)
Habit 9 : 73
Men and women 87 : 694
Self-awareness 109 : 859

Sutton, Jan
English author, counsellor (1945)
Listening 27 : 221
Self-esteem 111 : 876

Swindoll, Charles
US theologian, author (1934)
Attitude 16 : 133; 17 : 144; 18 : 146
Children and childhood 72 : 579

Szasz, Thomas
Hungarian-born US psychiatrist (1920)
Boredom 49 : 388
Neurosis and psychosis 89 : 711
Selfishness 112 : 881

Sex and sexual innuendo
114 : 903
Suicide 119 : 943

Taylor, Elizabeth
English-born US actress (1932)
Success 118 : 929

Temple, Sir William
English diplomat, essayist (1628–1699)
Humility 65 : 529

Tennyson, Alfred, Lord
English poet (1809–1892)
Eyes 42 : 336
Self-growth 111 :877

Thatcher, Margaret
English prime minister (1925)
Satisfaction 5 : 38
Talking 28 : 232
Determination 33 : 269
Feelings and emotions – general 46 : 361
Men and women 87 : 691
Patience 97 : 766
Money 100 : 794
Success 118 : 933

Tomlin, Lily
US actress, comedienne (1939)
Sanity and insanity 90 : 720
Reality 106 : 836

Tournier, Paul
Swiss doctor, psychotherapist, author (1898–1986)
Acceptance 3 : 23 4 : 25
Loneliness 54 : 437
Marriage 60 : 487
Self-development 111 : 873

Subject index